E. M. FORSTER

Edward Morgan Forster was born on January 1, 1879, in London and was raised from infancy by his mother and paternal aunts after his father's death. Forster's boyhood experiences at the Tonbridge School, Kent, were an unpleasant contrast to the happiness he found at home, and his suffering left him with an abiding dislike of the English public school system. At King's College, Cambridge, however, he was able to pursue freely his varied interests in philosophy, literature, and Mediterranean civilization, and he soon determined to devote his life to writing.

His first two novels were *Where Angels Fear to Tread* (1905) and *The Longest Journey* (1907), but it was not until the publication of *Howards End*, in 1910, that Forster achieved major success as a novelist.

Forster first visited India during 1912 and 1913, and after three years as a noncombatant in Alexandria, Egypt, during World War I and several years in England, he returned to India for an extended visit in 1921. From these experiences came his most celebrated novel, *A Passage to India*, his darkest and most probing work and perhaps the best novel about India written by a foreigner.

As a man of letters, Forster was honored during and after World War II for his resistance to any and all forms of tyranny and totalitarianism, and King's College awarded him a permanent fellowship in 1946. Forster spent his later years at Cambridge, writing and teaching, and died at Coventry, England, on June 7, 1970. His novel *Maurice*, written several decades earlier, was published posthumously in 1971.

Where Angels Fear to Tread

BY

E. M. FORSTER

*With an Introduction
by Jeffrey Meyers*

BANTAM BOOKS

NEW YORK TORONTO LONDON SYDNEY AUCKLAND

A BANTAM CLASSIC

WHERE ANGELS FEAR
TO TREAD
A Bantam Classic Book / July 1996
PUBLISHING HISTORY
Where Angels Fear to Tread was first published in 1920.

Cover art: The Cashmere Shawl by John Singer Sargent, 1911. The Charles
Henry Hayden Fund, courtesy of the Museum of Fine Arts, Boston.

ISBN 0-553-21446-2

Published simultaneously in the United States and Canada

Bantam Books are published by Bantam Books, a division of Bantam
Doubleday Dell Publishing Group, Inc. Its trademark, consisting of the words
"Bantam Books" and the portrayal of a rooster, is Registered in U.S. Patent
and Trademark Office and in other countries. Marca Registrada. Bantam
Books, 1540 Broadway, New York, New York 10036.

PRINTED IN THE UNITED STATES OF AMERICA

OPM 0 9 8 7 6 5 4 3 2 1

Where Angels
Fear to Tread

Introduction

by Jeffrey Meyers

E. M. FORSTER stood, as he said of the Greek poet Constantine Cavafy, "at a slight angle to the universe" and that oblique stance made him an acute observer of human frailty. Shy in appearance, feeble yet intellectually brilliant, he had been mercilessly bullied at school. He became in adult life a physically unattractive homosexual who admired personal beauty and longed for handsome young lads. Literary friends thought he looked like the man who came to wind the clocks and, mocking his reticence and secrecy, called him the Mole.

In *Where Angels Fear to Tread* (1905) he satirized the complacent absurdities of suburban Tonbridge, Kent, where he had grown up and gone to school, as Sawston—the town of saws, or platitudes. His fictional Philip Herriton, a weak man, keenly conscious of his physical defects, has a good deal in common

with Forster. And Philip's intense hostility to his offi-
cious mother expresses some of Forster's irritation
with his own mother, with whom he lived until he
was sixty-six, when her death finally released him.
Like Forster, Philip is a tame, repressed man who
wants to be wild. He feels that Italy might provide
the necessary release.

Forster's novel was published in the Edwardian
era, when the British Empire dominated the entire
world. There had not been a major European war
since the Napoleonic age, and during this extraordinarily secure and confident period the upper-middle
classes—immediately recognizable by their grand de-
meanor, dress, and accent—lorded it over their inferiors (including all foreigners) and indulged in classic
English vices: pomposity, hypocrisy, arrogance, smug-
ness, and snobbery. Constricted by puritanical sexual
repression, by rigid class distinctions, and by the in-
violable rules of conventional behavior, many of the
more intellectual and sensitive English men and
women longed to burst the boundaries of their narrow existence and lead a freer, more expansive
emotional life.

Italy, an appealing alternative to England, encouraged the bolder spirits to fulfill this hope. English writers had lived and traveled in Italy from
Byron and Shelley at the beginning of the nineteenth
century to the Brownings and Landor at the end.
Dickens's *Pictures from Italy* (1846), Gissing's *By the
Ionian Sea* (1901), and James's *Italian Hours* (1909)
had praised not only the art and architecture but also
the sunshine, the natural beauty, the good food and

wine, the traditional life, and the pagan, primitive element of that vital country.

Forster's felicitous mixture of comedy and social satire follows the novelistic tradition of Jane Austen and George Meredith, and *Where Angels Fear to Tread,* his first novel, foreshadows many techniques and themes in his later work. Always keen to make a moral point, he self-consciously returns to the Victorian convention and makes intrusive authorial comments on the behavior of his characters. He also deflates established religion and respectable middle-class conventions. His novel is structured by a clash of opposing values (Sawston vs. Monteriano, Italy) and by a series of unresolved moral ambiguities. Forster cannot convincingly describe passionate love between a man and a woman (when he tries to do so, he lapses into romantic clichés). But he is very good at portraying the dead marriage of Gino Carella and Lilia Herriton, and at suggesting that the strongest physical and emotional bonds are between men. Forster emphasizes the physical attractiveness of men, and contrasts the earthy and sometimes brutish heroes, like Gino, to stiff English prigs like Philip Herriton.

The snobbish and bigoted Herritons unsuccessfully oppose Lilia's marriage for all the wrong reasons. They try (too late) to bribe Gino to break his engagement and, later on, to persuade him to surrender his baby. Forster's novel portrays an essentially witty and satiric contrast between the primitive Italians and the repressed English, between feeling and instinct and obedience to external forms. But it also has somber undercurrents, as the constraints of

Edwardian society suppress the wish for sexual freedom, and the conflict between smothered emotions
and physical longing has tragic results—the sudden
and unexpected deaths of a mother and child.

In the expeditious opening chapter of this
charming and clever novel, Lilia, a wealthy, thirty-
three-year-old widow and mother of a small daughter, Irma, leaves England, accompanied by a much
younger but more sensible chaperon, Caroline
Abbott. To discourage the attentions of an eager
suitor, Lilia is sent away for a year in Italy. Her
brother-in-law, Philip, sees her off in London with
the well-intentioned but ultimately dangerous advice
not to "go with that awful tourist idea that Italy's only
a museum of antiquities and art. Love and understand the Italians." Yet he himself maintains an essentially remote, aesthetic view of Italy, and returns to
the constrictions of Sawston. Soon afterward, when
Caroline announces Lilia's astonishing engagement to
Gino—who is not (as she claims) a member of the
Italian nobility but the son of a dentist (an odious
profession) in Monteriano—Philip is dispatched as a
Jamesian ambassador to bring her back to her senses
and to her old stultifying way of life.

Lilia's impulsive, irregular marriage reveals how
she and three other English characters (Philip, his
sister Harriet, and their friend Caroline), all named in
the opening paragraph of the novel, respond to the
intense experience of Italy. Mrs. Herriton, who never
leaves England and remains the most rigidly insular,
casually assumes the right to interfere in Lilia's personal affairs, to judge others by her own exalted
standards, and to impose her own provincial values

on other people. Having alienated Lilia from her mother, her suitor, and her daughter, Mrs. Herriton now exclaims: "If Lilia marries him she insults the memory of [her late husband] Charles, she insults Irma, she insults us. Therefore I forbid her, and if she disobeys we have done with her forever."

Two opposing sets of values—social dictates against the wisdom of the heart—are immediately placed on a collision course as Philip enacts the title of the novel, which comes from Alexander Pope's *Essay on Criticism* (1711): "Fools rush in where angels fear to tread." Caroline Abbott, the touchstone of decent feelings, hates "the idleness, the stupidity, the respectability, the petty unselfishness" (trivial acts of charity) that characterize Sawston. And she, like all the English characters, is deeply moved by the revitalizing experience of Italy. In that pristine country people drink wine and are beautiful, and all natural, artistic, spiritual, and human aspects of the place— "olive-trees, blue sky, frescoes, country inns, saints, peasants, mosaics, statues, beggars"—merge into an aesthetic and humanistic whole.

Monteriano is modeled on a medieval Tuscan hill town, San Gimignano—twenty miles northwest of Siena—and the numerous towers, the Rocca, the Church of Sant' Agostino, and the Collegiate Church, all mentioned in the book, actually exist. The visionary painting of Santa Deodata, which Philip and Harriet gaze at in the middle of the novel, is in fact Domenico Ghirlandaio's fresco *St. Gregory Announces the Death of Santa Fina* (1475).

On his first visit Philip arrives in Monteriano too late to prevent the ill-fated marriage. When he tells the unrepentant Lilia that he has come to rescue her, she defies her "gallant defender." Fortified by her love, she pours out her long-suppressed resentment in a vitriolic speech: "For twelve years you've trained me and tortured me, and I'll stand it no more. . . . When I came to your house a poor young bride, how you all looked me over—never a kind word—and discussed me, and thought I might just do; and your mother corrected me, and your sister snubbed me, and you said funny things about me to show how clever you were. . . . [But] I can stand up against the world now, for I've found Gino, and this time I marry for love!" The cruel cut of "this time" reveals that she did not love Philip's brother. When Philip (echoing his mother) shrieks: "I forbid you to marry Carella," Gino suddenly appears and rejects Philip's feeble attempt at bribery. Then, in a fine dramatic reversal, he announces that they are already married and pushes the startled Philip onto the bed.

Gino, in fact, has married the older Lilia for her money, and soon becomes a tyrannical and adulterous husband. He idles away his time with his cronies, forbids her to take walks by herself, and virtually imprisons her at home. When she opposes his wishes, he threatens to hurt her. But Philip is fascinated by the coarse, brutish yet somehow attractive character of Gino, and their meeting reveals the strength of male bonds. Forster refers to the intense male friendship of the biblical David and Jonathan (1 Sam. 20:18), and stresses the transfiguring power of male love. When talking to Gino, his friend Spiridione misogynistically remarks: "*Sono poco simpatiche le donne* [*women are not congenial]. And the time we waste over them is much." Philip tells Caroline Abbott, with a significant qualification, that the desire to have children "is the strongest desire that can come to a man—if it comes to him at all." And Caroline, having for the first time awakened Philip's emotions, tells him: "she has not been good to you—your mother." All these remarks point to the covert homosexual theme in the novel.

On his second visit, Gino's temptation of Philip, who distrusts emotion, is subtle and complex, for both men have a homosexual element in their nature. Their sadomasochistic connection builds up to a crescendo of pain through a series of hints and touches. At the opera Philip is enchanted by the light caress of Carella's arm across his back, in the café Gino lays a sympathetic hand on Philip's knee, when Philip tells Gino of the baby's death he touches him on the shoulder for consolation. Philip is bound to Gino "by the ties of almost alarming intimacy" and confesses to Caroline: "I love him too!"

Gino, who also expresses the procreative urge, arouses the love of both Lilia and Caroline; and Philip is drawn to Caroline through his love for Gino. Lilia had, rather surprisingly, left her fatherless daughter with the "beastly Herritons" for an entire year and subjected her to the malign influence of their values, which she despised. She then hoped to compensate for the loss of her own child and to bind herself to the unfaithful Gino by bearing his son. The malice of Philip's spinster sister Harriet also derives in part from maternal frustration. The three women in the novel represent progressive stages of love: Harriet is completely repressed, Caroline is awakened but unfulfilled. Lilia is happy for a few months before her pitiful disillusionment with Gino, and must accept the bitter fact that Mrs. Herriton's dire predictions have come true,

Caroline, who also feels a passionate though repressed love for Gino, encouraged Lilia to marry him. After Gino becomes oppressive and unfaithful, and Lilia dies giving birth to his son, Caroline makes a second trip to Monteriano, followed this time by Philip and Harriet, to undo the "evil" and to rescue the infant, as Philip had once tried to rescue the mother. On this second journey Caroline imitates Lilia by falling in love with Gino, and Harriet takes up Caroline's role as guardian of Sawston's values. Philip, who changes most radically, comes under the sway of Italy and of Gino, and rejects his mother's mores.

But the meddlesome English do not understand that "wicked people are capable of love" and that Gino, with all his defects of character, adores his son. The second expedition, like the first, ends in failure. The "duel" in Sawston over Irma had foreshadowed the struggle over Lilia's baby in Monteriano. The Herritons first prevent Lilia from writing to Irma, then try to prevent Gino from bringing up his own son. They want to turn Gino's happy baby into a stifled child like Irma and into a miserable man like Philip. The difficult moral choice, as Caroline tells Philip (unaware of the irony of "brought up well"), is: "Do you want the child to stop with his father, who loves him and will bring him up badly, or do you want him to come to

Sawston, where no one loves him, but where he will be brought up well?"

Forster contrasts two distinct approaches to life and to art: the expert and sterile, sanctified by Mrs. Herriton and by Karl Baedeker's German guidebooks, and the emotional and intuitive, employed by those liberated English who have abandoned themselves to the experience of the exquisite peninsula. On the night before their momentous confrontation with Gino, Philip, Caroline, and Harriet go to the opera in Monteriano. Donizetti's *Lucia di Lammermoor*, based on the novel by Walter Scott, dramatizes the heroine's thwarted passion, madness, murder of her husband, and death. The violent waves of excitement that sweep around the theater threaten Harriet, who tries to stifle the audience. She is struck in the chest by the soprano's bouquet and storms out of the place. But the lively atmosphere makes Philip and Caroline more emotionally responsive to Italy, to Gino, and to each other.

Forster subtly uses Ghirlandaio's painting of Santa Fina to suggest the symbols, reveal the characters, and emphasize the themes of the book. The fresco of Santa Deodata (whose name means "given to God")—described at some length in chapter 6, when Philip and Harriet visit the Collegiate Church—is actually based on the life of the young Santa Fina (1238–53). She was renowned for the perfect resignation with which she accepted physical suffering, and her terrible bodily ailments expiated the sins of her townsfolk. In childhood she had been suddenly attacked by diseases and, according to the *Lives of the Saints*, "for five years was obliged to lie on one side without turning; that side became a mass of corruption, and she was eaten by worms and mice. . . . When her body was removed from the board on which it had rested, the rotten wood was found to be covered with white violets. . . . Many miracles were reported as having been wrought through her intercession."

Ghirlandaio's fresco is on the wall of the saint's chapel in the Collegiate Church at San Gimignano. In this painting the emaciated Fina lies on a plank bed on the bare floor, attended by her mother and her friend Beldia. Her rigid posture is emphasized by the horizontal lines of the long wooden table, with a copper pot, pomegranates, and wine, and by the paneled ceiling, supported by decorated columns. The enticing Tuscan landscape appears through the door and windows on both sides of St. Gregory, who appears in papal raiment, surrounded by six winged angels, to announce the end of her agony. The diagonal from Gregory to the heads of the two nurses reiterates the fixed gaze of the three women, who stare upward at the astonishing vision.

Each of the major characters in the novel reflects an aspect of the life of Santa Fina. The young Lilia, stretched out in bed and martyred by illness like Fina, dies in an exemplary and expiatory fashion. Philip also stands outside life instead of being positively engaged in it. Harriet has Fina's rather joyless religion; the virginal Caroline shares her renunciation of physical love. Her rescue of Philip, when Gino is twisting his broken arm, is the fictional equivalent of Fina's miraculous cure of Beldia's paralyzed arm. Even the ghastly town idiot, who brings Harriet's message to Philip, has—like Fina—"visions of the saints."

Ghirlandaio's frescò, like Donizetti's opera, provides an aesthetic model for *Where Angels Fear to Tread*. The novel's characters see Italy as a pageant and a spectacle, and it is composed in a series of operatic and dramatic scenes. One of the subtlest moments in the book takes place when Caroline visits Gino to discuss the disposition of the baby. As she waits for him in the darkened parlor, he enters the bedroom and (unaware of her presence) talks to his son while she voyeuristically observes him. She screams when he discovers her, and he too is frightened. As Forster perceptively observes: "It is a serious thing to have been watched. We all radiate something curiously intimate when we believe ourselves to be alone."

Just after Caroline and Gino have bathed the baby, and at the crucial moment when she realizes that she loves him, he places the infant on her knee and then kneels beside them. Philip, upon entering the villa, sees that they form a composition that is at once theatrical, artistic, and religious: "There she sat, with twenty miles of view behind her, and he placed the dripping baby on her knee. It shone now with health and beauty; it seemed to reflect light, like a copper vessel [used to bathe the baby]. . . . For a time Gino contemplated them standing. Then, to get a better view, he knelt by the side of the chair, with his hands clasped before him. So they were when Philip entered, and saw, to all intents and purposes, the Virgin and Child, with Donor."

When Philip intrudes on Caroline's sacred moment with Gino, who she had hoped would propose marriage, she bursts into tears and rushes out of the room.

Angered by Philip's failure to secure the baby, Harriet—with the help of the idiot-messenger, who paradoxically "understands everything, but can explain nothing"—steals the baby from Gino's house, tries to escape with it, and comes to disaster when the carriage overturns. After Philip tells Gino that he must scream and curse to release his feelings, the grief-stricken father brutally twists Philip's arm, broken in the accident that killed the baby, and makes him suffer excruciating agony: "The whole arm seemed red-hot, and the broken bone grated in the joint, sending out shoots of the essence of pain." Philip (in contrast to Santa Fina) responds melodramatically, as if he were a maiden threatened by a vile seducer, and exclaims: "You brute! . . . Kill me if you like! But just you leave my broken arm alone." This sadistic fight expresses their sexual passion and, after they are reconciled, allows Philip to achieve intimacy with his beloved by sharing his tragedy and bereavement.

Philip is rescued by Caroline, who takes him in her arms and holds him, as in "great pictures" when Mary cradles the dead Christ in a *pietà*. At this moment Philip, tortured and comforted, "underwent conversion" and is saved. To mark his transfiguration (a crucial word in Forster's novels), he ritualistically completes the symbolic baptism of the baby in the washing scene and takes symbolic Communion by drinking the baby's milk. Gino, in a rather surprising act of forgiveness, lies at the inquest to save Harriet from going to prison for kidnapping and manslaughter. In the final scene of the novel, on the train back to England, the symbolic violets that appear in the saint's legend and renew the miracle of spring every March form part of the cluster of images that Philip associates with the paradisal aspects of Italy: "That laughter in the theatre, those silver stars in the purple sky, even the violets of a departed spring, all had helped [bring him together with Caroline], and sorrow had helped also, and so had tenderness to others." This scene completes their three moments of sympathetic connection: at the opera, in Gino's villa, in the church. As Philip, with considerable difficulty, brings himself to the point of proposing marriage, Caroline surprises him by exclaiming that she is passionately attracted to Gino, and again bursts into hysterical tears, preferring genuine if frustrated feeling to a dead substitute for the real thing.

The novelist Rose Macaulay, in her book on Forster, calls *Where Angels Fear to Tread* "the story of the conquest of commonplace suburban, English respectability by Italian charm, by cheerful, graceful and rather brutal paganism." But the English characters who fall in love in Italy cannot surrender themselves to that glorious experience and are forced back into their desiccated existence. Sawston values triumph and their "conversion" remains incomplete. Italy has revealed that their lives are empty, but they cannot escape their frustration and doom.

Where Angels
Fear to Tread

Chapter One

THEY WERE ALL at Charing Cross to see Lilia off—Philip, Harriet, Irma, Mrs. Herriton herself. Even Mrs. Theobald, squired by Mr. Kingcroft, had braved the journey from Yorkshire to bid her only daughter good-bye. Miss Abbott was likewise attended by numerous relatives, and the sight of so many people talking at once and saying such different things caused Lilia to break into ungovernable peals of laughter.

"Quite an ovation," she cried, sprawling out of her first-class carriage. "They'll take us for royalty. Oh, Mr. Kingcroft, get us footwarmers."

The good-natured young man hurried away, and Philip, taking his place, flooded her with a final stream of advice and injunctions—where to stop, how to learn Italian, when to use mosquito-nets, what pictures to look at. "Remember," he concluded, "that it is only by going off the track that you get to know the country. See the little towns—Gubbio, Pienza, Cortona, San Gemignano, Monteriano. And don't, let me beg you, go with that awful tourist idea that Italy's only a museum of antiquities and art. Love and understand the Italians, for the people are more marvellous than the land."

"How I wish you were coming, Philip," she said, flattered at the unwonted notice her brother-in-law was giving her.

"I wish I were." He could have managed it without great difficulty, for his career at the Bar was not so intense as to prevent occasional holidays. But his family disliked his continual visits to the Continent, and he himself often found pleasure in the idea that he was too busy to leave town.

"Good-bye, dear every one. What a whirl!" She caught sight of her little daughter Irma, and felt that a touch of maternal solemnity was required. "Good-bye, darling. Mind you're always good, and do what Granny tells you."

She referred not to her own mother, but to her mother-in-law, Mrs. Herriton, who hated the title of Granny.

Irma lifted a serious face to be kissed, and said cautiously, "I'll do my best."

"She is sure to be good," said Mrs. Herriton, who was standing pensively a little out of the hubbub. But Lilia was already calling to Miss Abbott, a tall, grave, rather nice-looking young lady who was conducting her adieus in a more decorous manner on the platform.

"Caroline, my Caroline! Jump in, or your chaperon will go off without you."

And Philip, whom the idea of Italy always intoxicated, had started again, telling her of the supreme moments of her coming journey—the Campanile of Airolo, which would burst on her when she emerged from the St. Gothard tunnel, presaging the future; the view of the Ticino and Lago Maggiore as the train climbed the slopes of Monte Cenere; the view of Lugano, the view of Como—Italy gathering thick around her now—the arrival at her first resting-place, when, after long driving through dark and dirty streets, she should at last behold, amid the roar of trams and the glare of arc lamps, the buttresses of the cathedral of Milan.

"Handkerchiefs and collars," screamed Harriet, "in my inlaid box! I've lent you my inlaid box."

"Good old Harry!" She kissed every one again, and there was a moment's silence. They all smiled steadily, excepting Philip, who was choking in the fog, and old Mrs. Theobald, who had begun to cry. Miss Abbott got into the carriage. The guard himself shut the door, and told Lilia that she would be all right. Then the train moved, and they all moved with it a couple of steps, and waved their handkerchiefs, and uttered cheerful little cries. At that moment Mr. Kingcroft reappeared, carrying a footwarmer by both ends, as if it was a tea-tray. He was sorry that he was too late, and called out in a quivering voice, "Goodbye, Mrs. Charles. May you enjoy yourself, and may God bless you."

Lilia smiled and nodded, and then the absurd

position of the footwarmer overcame her, and she began to laugh again.

"Oh, I am so sorry," she cried back, "but you do look so funny. Oh, you all look so funny waving! Oh, pray!" And laughing helplessly, she was carried out into the fog.

"High spirits to begin so long a journey," said Mrs. Theobald, dabbing her eyes.

Mr. Kingcroft solemnly moved his head in token of agreement. "I wish," said he, "that Mrs. Charles had gotten the footwarmer. These London porters won't take heed to a country chap."

"But you did your best," said Mrs. Herriton. "And I think it simply noble of you to have brought Mrs. Theobald all the way here on such a day as this." Then, rather hastily, she shook hands, and left him to take Mrs. Theobald all the way back.

Sawston, her own home, was within easy reach of London, and they were not late for tea. Tea was in the dining-room, with an egg for Irma, to keep up the child's spirits. The house seemed strangely quiet after a fortnight's bustle, and their conversation was spasmodic and subdued. They wondered whether the travellers had got to Folkestone, whether it would be at all rough, and if so what would happen to poor Miss Abbott.

"And, Granny, when will the old ship get to Italy?" asked Irma.

"'Grandmother,' dear; not 'Granny,'" said Mrs. Herriton, giving her a kiss. "And we say 'a boat' or 'a steamer,' not 'a ship.' Ships have sails. And mother won't go all the way by sea. You look at the map of

Europe, and you'll see why. Harriet, take her. Go with Aunt Harriet, and she'll show you the map."

"Righto!" said the little girl, and dragged the reluctant Harriet into the library. Mrs. Herriton and her son were left alone. There was immediately confidence between them.

"Here beginneth the New Life," said Philip.

"Poor child, how vulgar!" murmured Mrs. Herriton. "It's surprising that she isn't worse. But she has got a look of poor Charles about her."

"And—alas, alas!—a look of old Mrs. Theobald. What appalling apparition was that! I did think the lady was bedridden as well as imbecile. Why ever did she come?"

"Mr. Kingcroft made her. I am certain of it. He wanted to see Lilia again, and this was the only way."

"I hope he is satisfied. I did not think my sister-in-law distinguished herself in her farewells."

Mrs. Herriton shuddered. "I mind nothing, so long as she has gone—and gone with Miss Abbott. It is mortifying to think that a widow of thirty-three requires a girl ten years younger to look after her."

"I pity Miss Abbott. Fortunately one admirer is chained to England. Mr. Kingcroft cannot leave the crops or the climate or something. I don't think, either, he improved his chances today. He, as well as Lilia, has the knack of being absurd in public."

Mrs. Herriton replied, "When a man is neither well bred, nor well connected, nor handsome, nor clever, nor rich, even Lilia may discard him in time."

"No. I believe she would take any one. Right up to the last, when her boxes were packed, she was 'playing' the chinless curate. Both the curates are chinless, but hers had the dampest hands. I came on them in the Park. They were speaking of the Penta-teuch."

"My dear boy! If possible, she has got worse and worse. It was your idea of Italian travel that saved us!"

Philip brightened at the little compliment. "The odd part is that she was quite eager—always asking me for information; and of course I was very glad to give it. I admit she is a Philistine, appallingly igno-rant, and her taste in art is false. Still, to have any taste at all is something. And I do believe that Italy really purifies and ennobles all who visit her. She is the school as well as the playground of the world. It is really to Lilia's credit that she wants to go there."

"She would go anywhere," said his mother, who had heard enough of the praises of Italy. "I and Caro-line Abbott had the greatest difficulty in dissuading her from the Riviera."

"No, mother; no. She was really keen on Italy. This travel is quite a crisis for her." He found the sit-uation full of whimsical romance: there was some-thing half attractive, half repellent in the thought of this vulgar woman journeying to places he loved and revered. Why should she not be transfigured? The same had happened to the Goths.

Mrs. Herriton did not believe in romance nor in transfiguration, nor in parallels from history, nor in anything else that may disturb domestic life. She adroitly changed the subject before Philip got ex-cited. Soon Harriet returned, having given her lesson in geography. Irma went to bed early, and was tucked up by her grandmother. Then the two ladies worked and played cards. Philip read a book. And so they all settled down to their quiet, profitable existence, and continued it without interruption through the winter.

It was now nearly ten years since Charles had fallen in love with Lilia Theobald because she was pretty, and during that time Mrs. Herriton had hardly known a moment's rest. For six months she schemed to prevent the match, and when it had taken place she turned to another task—the supervision of her daughter-in-law. Lilia must be pushed through life without bringing discredit on the family into which she had married. She was aided by Charles, by her daughter Harriet, and, as soon as he was old enough, by the clever one of the family, Philip. The birth of Irma made things still more difficult. But fortunately old Mrs. Theobald, who had attempted interference, began to break up. It was an effort to her to leave Whitby, and Mrs. Herriton discouraged the effort as far as possible. That curious duel which is fought over every baby was fought and decided early. Irma belonged to her father's family, not to her mother's.

Charles died, and the struggle recommenced. Lilia tried to assert herself, and said that she should go to take care of Mrs. Theobald. It required all Mrs. Herriton's kindness to prevent her. A house was finally taken for her at Sawston, and there for three years she lived with Irma, continually subject to the refining influences of her late husband's family.

During one of her rare Yorkshire visits trouble began again. Lilia confided to a friend that she liked a Mr. Kingcroft extremely, but that she was not exactly engaged to him. The news came round to Mrs. Herriton, who at once wrote, begging for information, and pointing out that Lilia must either be engaged or not, since no intermediate state existed. It was a good letter, and flurried Lilia extremely. She left Mr. Kingcroft without even the pressure of a rescue-party. She cried a great deal on her return to Sawston, and said she was very sorry. Mrs. Herriton took the opportunity of speaking more seriously about the duties of widowhood and motherhood than she had ever done before. But somehow things never went easily after. Lilia would not settle down in her place among Sawston matrons. She was a bad housekeeper, always in the throes of some domestic crisis, which Mrs. Herriton, who kept her servants for years, had to step across and adjust. She let Irma stop away from school for insufficient reasons, and she allowed her to wear rings. She learnt to bicycle, for the purpose of waking the place up, and coasted down the High Street one Sunday evening, falling off at the turn by the church. If she had not been a relative, it would have been entertaining. But even Philip, who in theory loved outraging English conventions, rose to the occasion, and gave her a talking which she remembered to her dying day. It was just then, too, that they discovered that she still allowed Mr. Kingcroft to write to her "as a gentleman friend," and to send presents to Irma.

Philip thought of Italy, and the situation was saved. Caroline, charming, sober, Caroline Abbott, who lived two turnings away, was seeking a companion for a year's travel. Lilia gave up her house, sold half her furniture, left the other half and Irma with Mrs. Herriton, and had now departed, amid universal approval, for a change of scene.

She wrote to them frequently during the winter—more frequently than she wrote to her mother. Her letters were always prosperous. Florence she found perfectly sweet, Naples a dream, but very whiffy. In Rome one had simply to sit still and feel. Philip, however, declared that she was improving. He was particularly gratified when in the early spring she began to visit the smaller towns that he had recommended. "In a place like this," she wrote, "one really does feel in the heart of things, and off the beaten track. Looking out of a Gothic window every morning, it seems impossible that the middle ages have passed away." The letter was from Monteriano, and concluded with a not unsuccessful description of the wonderful little town.

"It is something that she is contented," said Mrs. Herriton. "But no one could live three months with Caroline Abbott and not be the better for it."

Just then Irma came in from school, and she read her mother's letter to her, carefully correcting any grammatical errors, for she was a loyal supporter of parental authority. Irma listened politely, but soon changed the subject to hockey, in which her whole being was absorbed. They were to vote for colours that afternoon—yellow and white or yellow and green. What did her grandmother think?

Of course Mrs. Herriton had an opinion, which she sedately expounded, in spite of Harriet, who said that colours were unnecessary for children, and of Philip, who said that they were ugly. She was getting proud of Irma, who had certainly greatly improved, and could no longer be called that most appalling of things—a vulgar child. She was anxious to form her

before her mother returned. So she had no objection
to the leisurely movements of the travellers, and even
suggested that they should overstay their year if it
suited them.

Lilia's next letter was also from Monteriano, and
Philip grew quite enthusiastic.

"They've stopped there over a week!" he cried.
"Why! I shouldn't have done as much myself. They
must be really keen, for the hotel's none too comfortable."

"I cannot understand people," said Harriet.
"What can they be doing all day? And there is no
church there, I suppose."

"There is Santa Deodata, one of the most beautiful churches in Italy."

"Of course I mean an English church," said
Harriet stiffly. "Lilia promised me that she would always be in a large town on Sundays."

"If she goes to a service at Santa Deodata's, she
will find more beauty and sincerity than there is in
all the Back Kitchens of Europe."

The Back Kitchen was his nickname for St.
James's, a small depressing edifice much patronized
by his sister. She always resented any slight on it, and
Mrs. Herriton had to intervene.

"Now, dears, don't. Listen to Lilia's letter. 'We
love this place, and I do not know how I shall ever
thank Philip for telling me it. It is not only so quaint,
but one sees the Italians unspoiled in all their simplicity and charm here. The frescoes are wonderful.
Caroline, who grows sweeter every day, is very busy
sketching.' "

"Every one to his taste!" said Harriet, who always

delivered a platitude as if it was an epigram. She was curiously virulent about Italy, which she had never visited, her only experience of the Continent being an occasional six weeks in the Protestant parts of Switzerland.

"Oh, Harriet is a bad lot!" said Philip as soon as she left the room. His mother laughed, and told him not to be naughty; and the appearance of Irma, just off to school, prevented further discussion. Not only in Tracts is a child a peacemaker.

"One moment, Irma," said her uncle. "I'm going to the station. I'll give you the pleasure of my company."

They started together. Irma was gratified; but conversation flagged, for Philip had not the art of talking to the young. Mrs. Herriton sat a little longer at the breakfast table, re-reading Lilia's letter. Then she helped the cook to clear, ordered dinner, and started the housemaid turning out the drawing-room, Tuesday being its day. The weather was lovely, and she thought she would do a little gardening, as it was quite early. She called Harriet, who had recovered from the insult to St. James's, and together they went to the kitchen garden and began to sow some early vegetables.

"We will save the peas to the last; they are the greatest fun," said Mrs. Herriton, who had the gift of making work a treat. She and her elderly daughter always got on very well, though they had not a great deal in common. Harriet's education had been almost too successful. As Philip once said, she had "bolted all the cardinal virtues and couldn't digest them." Though pious and patriotic, and a great moral asset for the house, she lacked that pliancy and tact which her mother so much valued, and had expected her to pick up for herself. Harriet, if she had been allowed, would have driven Lilia to an open rupture, and, what was worse, she would have done the same to Philip two years before, when he returned full of passion for Italy, and ridiculing Sawston and its ways.

"It's a shame, mother!" she had cried. "Philip laughs at everything—the Book Club, the Debating Society, the Progressive Whist, the bazaars. People won't like it. We have our reputation. A house divided against itself cannot stand."

Mrs. Herriton replied in the memorable words, "Let Philip say what he likes, and he will let us do what we like." And Harriet had acquiesced.

They sowed the duller vegetables first, and a pleasant feeling of righteous fatigue stole over them as they addressed themselves to the peas. Harriet stretched a string to guide the row straight, and Mrs. Herriton scratched a furrow with a pointed stick. At the end of it she looked at her watch.

"It's twelve! The second post's in. Run and see if there are any letters."

Harriet did not want to go. "Let's finish the peas. There won't be any letters."

"No, dear; please go. I'll sow the peas, but you shall cover them up—and mind the birds don't see 'em!"

Mrs. Herriton was very careful to let those peas trickle evenly from her hand, and at the end of the row she was conscious that she had never sown better. They were expensive too.

"Actually old Mrs. Theobald!" said Harriet, returning.

"Read me the letter. My hands are dirty. How intolerable the crested paper is."

Harriet opened the envelope.

"I don't understand," she said; "it doesn't make sense."

"Her letters never did."

"But it must be sillier than usual," said Harriet, and her voice began to quaver. "Look here, read it, mother; I can't make head or tail."

Mrs. Herriton took the letter indulgently. "What is the difficulty?" she said after a long pause. "What is it that puzzles you in this letter?"

"The meaning——" faltered Harriet. The sparrows hopped nearer and began to eye the peas.

"The meaning is quite clear—Lilia is engaged to be married. Don't cry, dear; please me by not crying—don't talk at all. It's more than I could bear. She is going to marry some one she has met in a hotel. Take the letter and read for yourself." Suddenly she broke down over what might seem a small point. "How dare she not tell me direct! How dare she write first to Yorkshire! Pray, am I to hear through Mrs. Theobald—a patronizing, insolent letter like this? Have I no claim at all? Bear witness, dear"—she choked with passion—"bear witness that for this I'll never forgive her!"

"Oh, what is to be done?" moaned Harriet. "What is to be done?"

"This first!" She tore the letter into little pieces and scattered it over the mould. "Next, a telegram for

Lilia! No! a telegram for Miss Caroline Abbott. She, too, has something to explain."

"Oh, what is to be done?" repeated Harriet, as she followed her mother to the house. She was helpless before such effrontery. What awful thing—what awful person had come to Lilia? "Some one in the hotel." The letter only said that. What kind of person? A gentleman? An Englishman? The letter did not say.

"Wire reason of stay at Monteriano. Strange rumours," read Mrs. Herriton, and addressed the telegram to Abbott, Stella d'Italia, Monteriano, Italy. "If there is an office there," she added, "we might get an answer this evening. Since Philip is back at seven, and the eight-fifteen catches the midnight boat at Dover——Harriet, when you go with this, get £100 in £5 notes at the bank."

"Go, dear, at once; do not talk. I see Irma coming back; go quickly. . . . Well, Irma dear, and whose team are you in this afternoon—Miss Edith's or Miss May's?"

But as soon as she had behaved as usual to her grand-daughter, she went to the library and took out the large atlas, for she wanted to know about Monteriano. The name was in the smallest print, in the midst of a woolly-brown tangle of hills which were called the "Sub-Apennines." It was not so very far from Siena, which she had learnt at school. Past it there wandered a thin black line, notched at intervals like a saw, and she knew that this was a railway. But the map left a good deal to imagination, and she had not got any. She looked up the place in "Childe Harold," but Byron had not been there. Nor did

Mark Twain visit it in the "Tramp Abroad." The resources of literature were exhausted: she must wait till Philip came home. And the thought of Philip made her try Philip's room, and there she found "Central Italy," by Baedeker, and opened it for the first time in her life and read in it as follows:—

Monteriano (pop. 4800). Hotels: Stella d'Italia, moderate only; Globo, dirty. *Caffè Garibaldi. Post and Telegraph office in Corso Vittorio Emmanuele, next to theatre. Photographs at Seghena's (cheaper in Florence). Diligence (1 lira) meets principal trains.

Chief attractions (2–3 hours): Santa Deodata, Palazzo Pubblico, Sant' Agostino, Santa Caterina, Sant' Ambrogio, Palazzo Capocchi. Guide (2 lire) unnecessary. A walk round the Walls should on no account be omitted. The view from the Rocca (small gratuity) is finest at sunset.

History: Monteriano, the Mons Rianus of Antiquity, whose Ghibelline tendencies are noted by Dante (Purg. xx.), definitely emancipated itself from Poggibonsi in '261. Hence the distich, *"Poggibonizzi, fatti in là, che Monteriano si fa città!"* till recently enscribed over the Siena gate. It remained independent till 1530, when it was sacked by the Papal troops and became part of the Grand Duchy of Tuscany. It is now of small importance, and seat of the district prison. The inhabitants are still noted for their agreeable manners.

———

The traveller will proceed direct from the Siena gate to the Collegiate Church of Santa Deodata, and inspect (5th chapel on right) the charming * Frescoes. . . .

Mrs. Herriton did not proceed. She was not one to detect the hidden charms of Baedeker. Some of the information seemed to her unnecessary, all of it was dull. Whereas Philip could never read "The view from the Rocca (small gratuity) is finest at sunset" without a catching at the heart. Restoring the book to its place, she went downstairs, and looked up and down the asphalt paths for her daughter. She saw her at last, two turnings away, vainly trying to shake off Mr. Abbott, Miss Caroline Abbott's father. Harriet was always unfortunate. At last she returned, hot, agitated, crackling with bank-notes, and Irma bounced to greet her, and trod heavily on her corn.

"Your feet grow larger every day," said the agonized Harriet, and gave her niece a violent push. Then Irma cried, and Mrs. Herriton was annoyed with Harriet for betraying irritation. Lunch was nasty; and during pudding news arrived that the cook, by sheer dexterity, had broken a very vital knob off the kitchen-range. "It is too bad," said Mrs. Herriton. Irma said it was three bad, and was told not to be rude. After lunch Harriet would get out Baedeker, and read in injured tones about Monteriano, the Mons Rianus of Antiquity, till her mother stopped her.

"It's ridiculous to read, dear. She's not trying to marry any one in the place. Some tourist, obviously, who's stopping in the hotel. The place has nothing to do with it at all."

"But what a place to go to! What nice person, too, do you meet in a hotel?"

"Nice or nasty, as I have told you several times before, is not the point. Lilia has insulted our family, and she shall suffer for it. And when you speak against hotels, I think you forget that I met your father at Chamounix. You can contribute nothing, dear, at present, and I think you had better hold your tongue. I am going to the kitchen, to speak about the range."

She spoke just too much, and the cook said that if she could not give satisfaction she had better leave. A small thing at hand is greater than a great thing remote, and Lilia, misconducting herself upon a mountain in Central Italy, was immediately hidden. Mrs. Herriton flew to a registry office, failed; flew to another, failed again; came home, was told by the housemaid that things seemed so unsettled that she had better leave as well; had tea, wrote six letters, was interrupted by cook and housemaid, both weeping, asking her pardon, and imploring to be taken back. In the flush of victory the door-bell rang, and there was the telegram: "Lilia engaged to Italian nobility. Writing. Abbott."

"No answer," said Mrs. Herriton. "Get down Mr. Philip's Gladstone from the attic."

She would not allow herself to be frightened by the unknown. Indeed she knew a little now. The man was not an Italian noble, otherwise the telegram would have said so. It must have been written by Lilia. None but she would have been guilty of the fatuous vulgarity of "Italian nobility." She recalled phrases of this morning's letter: "We love this place— Caroline is sweeter than ever, and busy sketching— Italians full of simplicity and charm." And the remark of Baedeker, "The inhabitants are still noted for their agreeable manners," had a baleful meaning now. If Mrs. Herriton had no imagination, she had intuition, a more useful quality, and the picture she made to herself of Lilia's *fiancé* did not prove altogether wrong.

So Philip was received with the news that he must start in half an hour for Monteriano. He was in a painful position. For three years he had sung the praises of the Italians, but he had never contemplated having one as a relative. He tried to soften the thing down to his mother, but in his heart of hearts he agreed with her when she said, "The man may be a duke or he may be an organ-grinder. That is not the point. If Lilia marries him she insults the memory of Charles, she insults Irma, she insults us. Therefore I forbid her, and if she disobeys we have done with her for ever."

"I will do all I can," said Philip in a low voice. It was the first time he had had anything to do. He kissed his mother and sister and puzzled Irma. The hall was warm and attractive as he looked back into it from the cold March night, and he departed for Italy reluctantly, as for something commonplace and dull.

Before Mrs. Herriton went to bed she wrote to Mrs. Theobald, using plain language about Lilia's conduct, and hinting that it was a question on which every one must definitely choose sides. She added, as if it was an afterthought, that Mrs. Theobald's letter had arrived that morning.

Just as she was going upstairs she remembered that she never covered up those peas. It upset her more than anything, and again and again she struck the banisters with vexation. Late as it was, she got a lantern from the tool-shed and went down the garden to rake the earth over them. The sparrows had taken every one. But countless fragments of the letter remained, disfiguring the tidy ground.

Chapter Two

WHEN THE BEWILDERED tourist alights at the station of Monteriano, he finds himself in the middle of the country. There are a few houses round the railway, and many more dotted over the plain and the slopes of the hills, but of a town, mediaeval or otherwise, not the slightest sign. He must take what is suitably termed a "legno"—a piece of wood—and drive up eight miles of excellent road into the middle ages. For it is impossible, as well as sacrilegious, to be as quick as Baedeker.

It was three in the afternoon when Philip left the realms of common-sense. He was so weary with travelling that he had fallen asleep in the train. His fellow-passengers had the usual Italian gift of divination, and when Monteriano came they knew he wanted to go there, and dropped him out. His feet sank into the hot asphalt of the platform, and in a dream he watched the train depart, while the porter who ought to have been carrying his bag, ran up the line playing touch-you-last with the guard. Alas! he was in no humour for Italy. Bargaining for a legno bored him unutterably. The man asked six lire; and though Philip knew that for eight miles it should scarcely be more than four, yet he was about to give what he was asked, and so make the man discontented and unhappy for the rest of the day. He was saved from this social blunder by loud shouts, and looking up the road saw one cracking his whip and waving his reins and driving two horses furiously, and behind him there appeared the swaying figure of a woman, holding star-fish fashion on to anything she could touch. It was Miss Abbott, who had just received his letter from Milan announcing the time of his arrival, and had hurried down to meet him.

He had known Miss Abbott for years, and had never had much opinion about her one way or the other. She was good, quiet, dull, and amiable, and young only because she was twenty-three: there was nothing in her appearance or manner to suggest the fire of youth. All her life had been spent at Sawston with a dull and amiable father, and her pleasant, pallid face, bent on some respectable charity, was a familiar object of the Sawston streets. Why she had ever wished to leave them was surprising; but as she truly said, "I am John Bull to the backbone, yet I do want to see Italy, just once. Everybody says it is marvellous, and that one gets no idea of it from books at all." The curate suggested that a year was a long time; and Miss Abbott, with decorous playfulness, answered him, "Oh, but you must let me have my fling!

I promise to have it once, and once only. It will give me things to think about and talk about for the rest of my life." The curate had consented; so had Mr. Abbott. And here she was in a legno, solitary, dusty, frightened, with as much to answer and to answer for as the most dashing adventuress could desire.

They shook hands without speaking. She made room for Philip and his luggage amidst the loud indignation of the unsuccessful driver, whom it required the combined eloquence of the station-master and the station beggar to confute. The silence was prolonged until they started. For three days he had been considering what he should do, and still more what he should say. He had invented a dozen imaginary conversations, in all of which his logic and eloquence procured him certain victory. But how to begin? He was in the enemy's country, and everything—the hot sun, the cold air behind the heat, the endless rows of olive-trees, regular yet mysterious—seemed hostile to the placid atmosphere of Sawston in which his thoughts took birth. At the outset he made one great concession. If the match was really suitable, and Lilia were bent on it, he would give in, and trust to his influence with his mother to set things right. He would not have made the concession in England; but here in Italy, Lilia, however wilful and silly, was at all events growing to be a human being.

"Are we to talk it over now?" he asked.

"Certainly, please," said Miss Abbott, in great agitation. "If you will be so very kind."

"Then how long has she been engaged?"

Her face was that of a perfect fool—a fool in terror.

"A short time—quite a short time," she stammered, as if the shortness of the time would reassure him.

"I should like to know how long, if you can remember."

She entered into elaborate calculations on her fingers. "Exactly eleven days," she said at last.

"How long have you been here?"

More calculations, while he tapped irritably with his foot. "Close on three weeks."

"Did you know him before you came?"

"No."

"Oh! Who is he?"

"A native of the place."

The second silence took place. They had left the plain now and were climbing up the outposts of the hills, the olive-trees still accompanying. The driver, a jolly fat man, had got out to ease the horses, and was walking by the side of the carriage.

"I understood they met at the hotel."

"It was a mistake of Mrs. Theobald's."

"I also understand that he is a member of the Italian nobility."

She did not reply.

"May I be told his name?"

Miss Abbott whispered "Carella." But the driver heard her, and a grin split over his face. The engagement must be known already.

"Carella? Conte or Marchese, or what?"

"Signor," said Miss Abbott, and looked helplessly aside.

"Perhaps I bore you with these questions. If so, I will stop."

"Oh, no, please; not at all. I am here—my own idea—to give all information which you very naturally—and to see if somehow—please ask anything you like."

"Then how old is he?"

"Oh, quite young. Twenty-one, I believe."

There burst from Philip the exclamation, "Good Lord!"

"One would never believe it," said Miss Abbott, flushing. "He looks much older."

"And is he good-looking?" he asked, with gathering sarcasm.

She became decisive. "Very good-looking. All his features are good, and he is well built—though I dare say English standards would find him too short."

Philip, whose one physical advantage was his height, felt annoyed at her implied indifference to it.

"May I conclude that you like him?"

She replied decisively again, "As far as I have seen him, I do."

At that moment the carriage entered a little wood, which lay brown and sombre across the cultivated hill. The trees of the wood were small and leafless, but noticeable for this—that their stems stood in violets as rocks stand in the summer sea. There are such violets in England, but not so many. Nor are there so many in Art, for no painter has the courage. The cart-ruts were channels, the hollow lagoons; even the dry white margin of the road was splashed, like a causeway soon to be submerged under the advancing tide of spring. Philip paid no attention at the time: he was thinking what to say next. But his eyes had registered the beauty, and next March he did not forget that the road to Monteriano must traverse innumerable flowers.

"As far as I have seen him, I do like him," repeated Miss Abbott, after a pause.

He thought she sounded a little defiant, and crushed her at once.

"What is he, please? You haven't told me that. What's his position?"

She opened her mouth to speak, and no sound came from it. Philip waited patiently. She tried to be audacious, and failed pitiably.

"No position at all. He is kicking his heels, as my father would say. You see, he has only just finished his military service."

"As a private?"

"I suppose so. There is general conscription. He was in the Bersaglieri, I think. Isn't that the crack regiment?"

"The men in it must be short and broad: They must also be able to walk six miles an hour."

She looked at him wildly, not understanding all that he said, but feeling that he was very clever. Then she continued her defence of Signor Carella.

"And now, like most young men, he is looking out for something to do."

"Meanwhile?"

"Meanwhile, like most young men, he lives with his people—father, mother, two sisters, and a tiny tot of a brother."

There was a grating sprightliness about her that

drove him nearly mad. He determined to silence her at last.

"One more question, and only one more. What is his father?"

"His father," said Miss Abbott. "Well, I don't suppose you'll think it a good match. But that's not the point. I mean the point is not—I mean that social differences—love, after all—not but what——"

Philip ground his teeth together and said nothing.

"Gentlemen sometimes judge hardly. But I feel that you, and at all events your mother—so really good in every sense, so really unworldly—after all, love—marriages are made in heaven."

"Yes, Miss Abbott, I know. But I am anxious to hear heaven's choice. You arouse my curiosity. Is my sister-in-law to marry an angel?"

"Mr. Herriton, don't—please, Mr. Herriton—a dentist. His father's a dentist."

Philip gave a cry of personal disgust and pain. He shuddered all over, and edged away from his companion. A dentist! A dentist at Monteriano. A dentist in fairyland! False teeth and laughing gas and the tilting chair at a place which knew the Etruscan League, and the Pax Romana, and Alaric himself, and the Countess Matilda, and the Middle Ages, all fighting and holiness, and the Renaissance, all fighting and beauty! He thought of Lilia no longer. He was anxious for himself: he feared that Romance might die.

Romance only dies with life. No pair of pincers will ever pull it out of us. But there is a spurious sentiment which cannot resist the unexpected and the incongruous and the grotesque. A touch will loosen it, and the sooner it goes from us the better. It was going from Philip now, and therefore he gave the cry of pain.

"I cannot think what is in the air," he began. "If Lilia was determined to disgrace us, she might have found a less repulsive way. A boy of medium height with a pretty face, the son of a dentist at Monteriano. Have I put it correctly? May I surmise that he has not got one penny? May I also surmise that his social position is nil? Furthermore——"

"Stop! I'll tell you no more."

"Really, Miss Abbott, it is a little late for reticence. You have equipped me admirably!"

"I'll tell you not another word!" she cried, with a spasm of terror. Then she got out her handkerchief, and seemed as if she would shed tears. After a silence, which he intended to symbolize to her the dropping of a curtain on the scene, he began to talk of other subjects.

They were among olives again, and the wood with its beauty and wildness had passed away. But as they climbed higher the country opened out, and there appeared, high on a hill to the right, Monteriano. The hazy green of the olives rose up to its walls, and it seemed to float in isolation between trees and sky, like some fantastic ship city of a dream. Its colour was brown, and it revealed not a single house—nothing but the narrow circle of the walls, and behind them seventeen towers—all that was left of the fifty-two that had filled the city in her prime. Some were only stumps, some were inclining stiffly to their fall, some were still erect, piercing like masts into the blue. It was impossible to praise it as beautiful, but it was also impossible to damn it as quaint.

Meanwhile Philip talked continually, thinking this to be great evidence of resource and tact. It showed Miss Abbott that he had probed her to the bottom, but was able to conquer his disgust, and by sheer force of intellect continue to be as agreeable and amusing as ever. He did not know that he talked a good deal of nonsense, and that the sheer force of his intellect was weakened by the sight of Monteriano, and by the thought of dentistry within those walls.

The town above them swung to the left, to the right, to the left again, as the road wound upward through the trees, and the towers began to glow in the descending sun. As they drew near, Philip saw the heads of people gathering black upon the walls, and he knew well what was happening—how the news was spreading that a stranger was in sight, and the beggars were aroused from their content and bid to adjust their deformities; how the alabaster man was running for his wares, and the Authorized Guide running for his peaked cap and his two cards of recommendation—one from Miss M'Gee, Maida Vale, the other, less valuable, from an Equerry to the Queen of Peru; how some one else was running to tell the landlady of the Stella d'Italia to put on her pearl necklace and brown boots and empty the slops from the spare bedroom; and how the landlady was running to tell Lilia and her boy that their fate was at hand.

Perhaps it was a pity Philip had talked so profusely. He had driven Miss Abbott half demented, but he had given himself no time to concert a plan. The end came so suddenly. They emerged from the trees on to the terrace before the walk, with the vision of half Tuscany radiant in the sun behind them, and then they turned in through the Siena gate, and their journey was over. The Dogana men admitted them with an air of gracious welcome, and they clattered up the narrow dark street, greeted by that mixture of curiosity and kindness which makes each Italian arrival so wonderful.

He was stunned and knew not what to do. At the hotel he received no ordinary reception. The landlady wrung him by the hand; one person snatched his umbrella, another his bag; people pushed each other out of his way. The entrance seemed blocked with a crowd. Dogs were barking, bladder whistles being blown, women waving their handkerchiefs, excited children screaming on the stairs, and at the top of the stairs was Lilia herself, very radiant, with her best blouse on.

"Welcome!" she cried. "Welcome to Monteriano!" He greeted her, for he did not know what else to do, and a sympathetic murmur rose from the crowd below.

"You told me to come here," she continued, "and I don't forget it. Let me introduce Signor Carella!"

Philip discerned in the corner behind her a young man who might eventually prove handsome and well-made, but certainly did not seem so then. He was half enveloped in the drapery of a cold dirty curtain, and nervously stuck out a hand, which Philip took and found thick and damp. There were more murmurs of approval from the stairs.

"Well, din-din's nearly ready," said Lilia. "Your room's down the passage, Philip. You needn't go changing."

He stumbled away to wash his hands, utterly crushed by her effrontery.

"Dear Caroline!" whispered Lilia as soon as he had gone. "What an angel you've been to tell him! He takes it so well. But you must have had a *mauvais quart d'heure*."

Miss Abbott's long terror suddenly turned into acidity. "I've told nothing," she snapped. "It's all for you—and if it only takes a quarter of an hour you'll be lucky!"

Dinner was a nightmare. They had the smelly dining-room to themselves. Lilia, very smart and vociferous, was at the head of the table; Miss Abbott, also in her best, sat by Philip, looking, to his irritated nerves, more like the tragedy confidante every moment. That scion of the Italian nobility, Signor Carella, sat opposite. Behind him loomed a bowl of goldfish, who swam round and round, gaping at the guests.

The face of Signor Carella was twitching too much for Philip to study it. But he could see the hands, which were not particularly clean, and did not get cleaner by fidgeting amongst the shining slabs of hair. His starched cuffs were not clean either, and as for his suit, it had obviously been bought for the occasion as something really English—a gigantic check, which did not even fit. His handkerchief he had forgotten, but never missed it. Altogether, he was quite unpresentable, and very lucky to have a father who was a dentist in Monteriano. And why, even

Lilia—— But as soon as the meal began it furnished Philip with an explanation.

For the youth was hungry, and his lady filled his plate with spaghetti, and when those delicious slippery worms were flying down his throat, his face relaxed and became for a moment unconscious and calm. And Philip had seen that face before in Italy a hundred times—seen it and loved it, for it was not merely beautiful, but had the charm which is the rightful heritage of all who are born on that soil. But he did not want to see it opposite him at dinner. It was not the face of a gentleman.

Conversation, to give it that name, was carried on in a mixture of English and Italian. Lilia had picked up hardly any of the latter language, and Signor Carella had not yet learnt any of the former. Occasionally Miss Abbott had to act as interpreter between the lovers, and the situation became uncouth and revolting in the extreme. Yet Philip was too cowardly to break forth and denounce the engagement. He thought he should be more effective with Lilia if he had her alone, and pretended to himself that he must hear her defence before giving judgment.

Signor Carella, heartened by the spaghetti and the throat-rasping wine, attempted to talk, and, looking politely towards Philip, said, "England is a great country. The Italians love England and the English."

Philip, in no mood for international amenities, merely bowed.

"Italy too," the other continued a little resentfully, "is a great country. She has produced many famous men—for example Garibaldi and Dante. The latter

wrote the 'Inferno,' the 'Purgatorio,' the 'Paradiso.'
The 'Inferno' is the most beautiful." And with the
complacent tone of one who has received a solid
education, he quoted the opening lines—

> Nel mezzo del cammin di nostra vita
> Mi ritrovai per una selva oscura
> Che la diritta via era smarrita—

a quotation which was more apt than he supposed.

Lilia glanced at Philip to see whether he noticed
that she was marrying no ignoramus. Anxious to ex-
hibit all the good qualities of her betrothed, she abruptly introduced the subject of pallone, in which, it
appeared, he was a proficient player. He suddenly became shy and developed a conceited grin—the grin
of the village yokel whose cricket score is mentioned
before a stranger. Philip himself had loved to watch
pallone, that entrancing combination of lawn-tennis
and fives. But he did not expect to love it quite so
much again.

"Oh, look!" exclaimed Lilia, "the poor wee fish!"

A starved cat had been worrying them all for
pieces of the purple quivering beef they were trying
to swallow. Signor Carella, with the brutality so common in Italians, had caught her by the paw and flung
her away from him. Now she had climbed up to the
bowl and was trying to hook out the fish. He got up,
drove her off, and finding a large glass stopper by the
bowl, entirely plugged up the aperture with it.

"But may not the fish die?" said Miss Abbott.
"They have no air."

"Fish live on water, not on air," he replied in a

knowing voice, and sat down. Apparently he was at his ease again, for he took to spitting on the floor. Philip glanced at Lilia but did not detect her wincing. She talked bravely till the end of the disgusting meal, and then got up saying, "Well, Philip, I am sure you are ready for by-bye. We shall meet at twelve o'clock lunch tomorrow, if we don't meet before. They give us *caffè* later in our rooms."

It was a little too impudent. Philip replied, "I should like to see you now, please, in my room, as I have come all the way on business." He heard Miss Abbott gasp. Signor Carella, who was lighting a rank cigar, had not understood.

It was as he expected. When he was alone with Lilia he lost all nervousness. The remembrance of his long intellectual supremacy strengthened him, and he began volubly—

"My dear Lilia, don't let's have a scene. Before I arrived I thought I might have to question you. It is unnecessary. I know everything. Miss Abbott has told me a certain amount, and the rest I see for myself."

"See for yourself?" she exclaimed, and he remembered afterwards that she had flushed crimson.

"That he is probably a ruffian and certainly a cad."

"There are no cads in Italy," she said quickly.

He was taken aback. It was one of his own remarks. And she further upset him by adding, "He is the son of a dentist. Why not?"

"Thank you for the information. I know everything, as I told you before. I am also aware of the social position of an Italian who pulls teeth in a minute provincial town."

He was not aware of it, but he ventured to conclude that it was pretty low. Nor did Lilia contradict him. But she was sharp enough to say, "Indeed, Philip, you surprise me. I understood you went in for equality and so on."

"And I understood that Signor Carella was a member of the Italian nobility."

"Well, we put it like that in the telegram so as not to shock dear Mrs. Herriton. But it is true. He is a younger branch. Of course families ramify—just as in yours there is your cousin Joseph." She adroitly picked out the only undesirable member of the Herriton clan. "Gino's father is courtesy itself, and rising rapidly in his profession. This very month he leaves Monteriano, and sets up at Poggibonsi. And for my own poor part, I think what people *are* is what matters, but I don't suppose you'll agree. And I should like you to know that Gino's uncle is a priest—the same as a clergyman at home."

Philip was aware of the social position of an Italian priest, and said so much about it that Lilia interrupted him with, "Well, his cousin's a lawyer at Rome."

"What kind of 'lawyer'?"

"Why, a lawyer just like you are—except that he has lots to do and can never get away."

The remark hurt more than he cared to show. He changed his method, and in a gentle, conciliating tone delivered the following speech:—

"The whole thing is like a bad dream—so bad that it cannot go on. If there was one redeeming feature about the man I might be uneasy. As it is I can trust to time. For the moment, Lilia, he has taken you in, but you will find him out soon. It is not possible that you, a lady, accustomed to ladies and gentlemen, will tolerate a man whose position is—well, not equal to the son of the servants' dentist in Coronation Place. I am not blaming you now. But I blame the glamour of Italy—I have felt it myself, you know—and I greatly blame Miss Abbott."

"Caroline! Why blame her? What's all this to do with Caroline?"

"Because we expected her to———" He saw that the answer would involve him in difficulties, and, waving his hand, continued, "So I am confident, and you in your heart agree, that this engagement will not last. Think of your life at home—think of Irma! And I'll also say think of us; for you know, Lilia, that we count you more than a relation. I should feel I was losing my own sister if you did this, and my mother would lose a daughter."

She seemed touched at last, for she turned away her face and said, "I can't break it off now!"

"Poor Lilia," said he, genuinely moved. "I know it may be painful. But I have come to rescue you, and, book-worm though I may be, I am not frightened to stand up to a bully. He's merely an insolent boy. He thinks he can keep you to your word by threats. He will be different when he sees he has a man to deal with."

What follows should be prefaced with some simile—the simile of a powder-mine, a thunderbolt, an earthquake—for it blew Philip up in the air and flattened him on the ground and swallowed him up in the depths. Lilia turned on her gallant defender and said—

"For once in my life I'll thank you to leave me alone. I'll thank your mother too. For twelve years you've trained me and tortured me, and I'll stand it no more. Do you think I'm a fool? Do you think I never felt? Ah! when I came to your house a poor young bride, how you all looked me over—never a kind word—and discussed me, and thought I might just do; and your mother corrected me, and your sister snubbed me, and you said funny things about me to show how clever you were! And when Charles died I was still to run in strings for the honour of your beastly family, and I was to be cooped up at Sawston and learn to keep house, and all my chances spoilt of marrying again. No, thank you! No, thank you! 'Bully?' 'Insolent boy?' Who's that, pray, but you? But, thank goodness, I can stand up against the world now, for I've found Gino, and this time I marry for love!"

The coarseness and truth of her attack alike overwhelmed him. But her supreme insolence found him words, and he too burst forth.

"Yes! and I forbid you to do it! You despise me, perhaps, and think I'm feeble. But you're mistaken. You are ungrateful and impertinent and contemptible, but I will save you in order to save Irma and our name. There is going to be such a row in this town that you and he'll be sorry you came to it. I shall shrink from nothing, for my blood is up. It is unwise of you to laugh. I forbid you to marry Carella, and I shall tell him so now."

"Do," she cried. "Tell him so now. Have it out with him. Gino! Gino! Come in! Avanti! Fra Filippo forbids the banns!"

Gino appeared so quickly that he must have been listening outside the door.

"Fra Filippo's blood's up. He shrinks from nothing. Oh, take care he doesn't hurt you!" She swayed about in vulgar imitation of Philip's walk, and then, with a proud glance at the square shoulders of her betrothed, flounced out of the room.

Did she intend them to fight? Philip had no intention of doing so; and no more, it seemed, had Gino, who stood nervously in the middle of the room with twitching lips and eyes.

"Please sit down, Signor Carella," said Philip in Italian. "Mrs. Herriton is rather agitated, but there is no reason we should not be calm. Might I offer you a cigarette? Please sit down."

He refused the cigarette and the chair, and remained standing in the full glare of the lamp. Philip, not averse to such assistance, got his own face into shadow.

For a long time he was silent. It might impress Gino, and it also gave him time to collect himself. He would not this time fall into the error of blustering, which he had caught so unaccountably from Lilia. He would make his power felt by restraint.

Why, when he looked up to begin, was Gino convulsed with silent laughter? It vanished immediately; but he became nervous, and was even more pompous than he intended.

"Signor Carella, I will be frank with you. I have come to prevent you marrying Mrs. Herriton, because I see you will both be unhappy together. She is English, you are Italian; she is accustomed to one

thing, you to another. And—pardon me if I say it—
she is rich and you are poor."

"I am not marrying her because she is rich," was
the sulky reply.

"I never suggested that for a moment," said
Philip courteously. "You are honourable, I am sure;
but are you wise? And let me remind you that we
want her with us at home. Her little daughter will be
motherless, our home will be broken up. If you grant
my request you will earn our thanks—and you will
not be without a reward for your disappointment."

"Reward—what reward?" He bent over the back
of a chair and looked earnestly at Philip. They were
coming to terms pretty quickly. Poor Lilia!

Philip said slowly, "What about a thousand lire?"

His soul went forth into one exclamation, and
then he was silent, with gaping lips. Philip would
have given double: he had expected a bargain.

"You can have them tonight."

He found words, and said, "It is too late."

"But why?"

"Because——" His voice broke. Philip watched
his face,—a face without refinement perhaps, but not
without expression,—watched it quiver and re-form
and dissolve from emotion into emotion. There was
avarice at one moment, and insolence, and politeness, and stupidity, and cunning—and let us hope
that sometimes there was love. But gradually one
emotion dominated, the most unexpected of all; for
his chest began to heave and his eyes to wink and his
mouth to twitch, and suddenly he stood erect and
roared forth his whole being in one tremendous
laugh.

Philip sprang up, and Gino, who had flung wide his arms to let the glorious creature go, took him by the shoulders and shook him, and said, "Because we are married—married—married as soon as I knew you were coming. There was no time to tell you. Oh, oh! You have come all the way for nothing. Oh! And oh, your generosity!" Suddenly he became grave, and said, "Please pardon me; I am rude. I am no better than a peasant, and I——" Here he saw Philip's face, and it was too much for him. He gasped and exploded and crammed his hands into his mouth and spat them out in another explosion, and gave Philip an aimless push, which toppled him on to the bed. He uttered a horrified Oh! and then gave up, and bolted away down the passage, shrieking like a child, to tell the joke to his wife.

For a time Philip lay on the bed, pretending to himself that he was hurt grievously. He could scarcely see for temper, and in the passage he ran against Miss Abbott, who promptly burst into tears.

"I sleep at the Globo," he told her, "and start for Sawston tomorrow morning early. He has assaulted me. I could prosecute him. But shall not."

"I can't stop here," she sobbed. "I daren't stop here. You will have to take me with you!"

Chapter Three

OPPOSITE THE VOLTERRA gate of Monteriano, outside the city, is a very respectable white-washed mud
wall, with a coping of red crinkled tiles to keep it
from dissolution. It would suggest a gentleman's garden if there was not in its middle a large hole, which
grows larger with every rain-storm. Through the hole
is visible, firstly, the iron gate that is intended to close
it; secondly, a square piece of ground which, though
not quite mud, is at the same time not exactly grass;
and finally, another wall, stone this time, which has
a wooden door in the middle and two wooden-
shuttered windows each side, and apparently forms
the façade of a one-storey house.

This house is bigger than it looks, for it slides for
two storeys down the hill behind, and the wooden
door, which is always locked, really leads into the attic. The knowing person prefers to follow the precipi-

tous mule-track round the turn of the mud wall till he can take the edifice in the rear. Then—being now on a level with the cellars—he lifts up his head and shouts. If his voice sounds like something light—a letter, for example, or some vegetables, or a bunch of flowers—a basket is let out of the first-floor windows by a string, into which he puts his burdens and departs. But if he sounds like something heavy, such as a log of wood, or a piece of meat, or a visitor, he is interrogated, and then bidden or forbidden to ascend. The ground floor and the upper floor of that battered house are alike deserted, and the inmates keep to the central portion, just as in a dying body all life retires to the heart. There is a door at the top of the first flight of stairs, and if the visitor is admitted he will find a welcome which is not necessarily cold. There are several rooms, some dark and mostly stuffy—a reception-room adorned with horsehair chairs, wool-work stools, and a stove that is never lit—German bad taste without German domesticity broods over that room; also a living-room, which insensibly glides into a bedroom when the refining influence of hospitality is absent, and real bedrooms; and last, but not least, the loggia, where you can live day and night if you feel inclined, drinking vermouth and smoking cigarettes, with leagues of olive-trees and vineyards and blue-green hills to watch you.

It was in this house that the brief and inevitable tragedy of Lilia's married life took place. She made Gino buy it for her, because it was there she had first seen him sitting on the mud wall that faced the Volterra gate. She remembered how the evening sun had struck his hair, and how he had smiled down at her, and being both sentimental and unrefined, was determined to have the man and the place together. Things in Italy are cheap for an Italian, and, though he would have preferred a house in the piazza, or better still a house at Siena, or, bliss above bliss, a house at Leghorn, he did as she asked, thinking that perhaps she showed her good taste in preferring so retired an abode.

The house was far too big for them, and there was a general concourse of his relatives to fill it up. His father wished to make it a patriarchal concern, where all the family should have their rooms and meet together for meals, and was perfectly willing to give up the new practice at Poggibonsi and preside. Gino was quite willing too, for he was an affectionate youth who liked a large home-circle, and he told it as a pleasant bit of news to Lilia, who did not attempt to conceal her horror.

At once he was horrified too; saw that the idea was monstrous; abused himself to her for having suggested it; rushed off to tell his father that it was impossible. His father complained that prosperity was already corrupting him and making him unsympathetic and hard; his mother cried; his sisters accused him of blocking their social advance. He was apologetic, and even cringing, until they turned on Lilia. Then he turned on them, saying that they could not understand, much less associate with, the English lady who was his wife; that there should be one master in that house—himself.

Lilia praised and petted him on his return, calling him brave and a hero and other endearing epithets. But he was rather blue when his clan left

Monteriano in much dignity—a dignity which was not at all impaired by the acceptance of a cheque. They took the cheque not to Poggibonsi, after all, but to Empoli—a lively, dusty town some twenty miles off. There they settled down in comfort, and the sisters said they had been driven to it by Gino.

The cheque was, of course, Lilia's, who was extremely generous, and was quite willing to know anybody so long as she had not to live with them, relations-in-law being on her nerves. She liked nothing better than finding out some obscure and distant connection—there were several of them—and acting the lady bountiful, leaving behind her bewilderment, and too often discontent. Gino wondered how it was that all his people, who had formerly seemed so pleasant, had suddenly become plaintive and disagreeable. He put it down to his lady-wife's magnificence, in comparison with which all seemed common. Her money flew apace, in spite of the cheap living. She was even richer than he expected; and he remembered with shame how he had once regretted his inability to accept the thousand lire that Philip Herriton offered him in exchange for her. It would have been a short-sighted bargain.

Lilia enjoyed settling into the house, with nothing to do except give orders to smiling workpeople, and a devoted husband as interpreter. She wrote a jaunty account of her happiness to Mrs. Herriton, and Harriet answered the letter, saying (1) that all future communications should be addressed to the solicitors; (2) would Lilia return an inlaid box which Harriet had lent her—but not given—to keep handkerchiefs and collars in?

"Look what I am giving up to live with you!" she said to Gino, never omitting to lay stress on her condescension. He took her to mean the inlaid box, and said that she need not give it up at all.

"Silly fellow, no! I mean the life. Those Herritons are very well connected. They lead Sawston society. But what do I care, so long as I have my silly fellow!" She always treated him as a boy, which he was, and as a fool, which he was not, thinking herself so immeasurably superior to him that she neglected opportunity after opportunity of establishing her rule. He was good-looking and indolent; therefore he must be stupid. He was poor; therefore he would never dare to criticize his benefactress. He was passionately in love with her; therefore she could do exactly as she liked.

"It mayn't be heaven below," she thought, "but it's better than Charles."

And all the time the boy was watching her, and growing up.

She was reminded of Charles by a disagreeable letter from the solicitors, bidding her disgorge a large sum of money for Irma, in accordance with her late husband's will. It was just like Charles's suspicious nature to have provided against a second marriage. Gino was equally indignant, and between them they composed a stinging reply, which had no effect. He then said that Irma had better come out and live with them. "The air is good, so is the food; she will be happy here, and we shall not have to part with the money." But Lilia had not the courage even to suggest this to the Herritons, and an unexpected terror seized her at the thought of Irma or any English child being educated at Monteriano.

Gino became terribly depressed over the solicitors' letter, more depressed than she thought necessary. There was no more to do in the house, and he spent whole days in the loggia leaning over the parapet or sitting astride it disconsolately.

"Oh, you idle boy!" she cried, pinching his muscles. "Go and play pallone."

"I am a married man," he answered, without raising his head. "I do not play games any more."

"Go and see your friends then."

"I have no friends now."

"Silly, silly, silly! You can't stop indoors all day!"

"I want to see no one but you." He spat on to an olive-tree.

"Now, Gino, don't be silly. Go and see your friends, and bring them to see me. We both of us like society."

He looked puzzled, but allowed himself to be persuaded, went out, found that he was not as friendless as he supposed, and returned after several hours in altered spirits. Lilia congratulated herself on her good management.

"I'm ready, too, for people now," she said. "I mean to wake you all up, just as I woke up Sawston. Let's have plenty of men—and make them bring their womenkind. I mean to have real English tea-parties."

"There is my aunt and her husband; but I thought you did not want to receive my relatives."

"I never said such a——"

"But you would be right," he said earnestly. "They are not for you. Many of them are in trade, and even we are little more; you should have gentle-folk and nobility for your friends."

"Poor fellow," thought Lilia. "It is sad for him to discover that his people are vulgar." She began to tell him that she loved him just for his silly self, and he flushed and began tugging at his moustache.

"But besides your relatives I must have other people here. Your friends have wives and sisters, haven't they?"

"Oh, yes; but of course I scarcely know them."

"Not know your friends' people?"

"Why, no. If they are poor and have to work for their living I may see them—but not otherwise. Except——" He stopped. The chief exception was a young lady, to whom he had once been introduced for matrimonial purposes. But the dowry had proved inadequate, and the acquaintance terminated.

"How funny! But I mean to change all that. Bring your friends to see me, and I will make them bring their people."

He looked at her rather hopelessly.

"Well, who are the principal people here? Who leads society?"

The governor of the prison, he supposed, and the officers who assisted him.

"Well, are they married?"

"Yes."

"There we are. Do you know them?"

"Yes—in a way."

"I see," she exclaimed angrily. "They look down on you, do they, poor boy? Wait!" He assented. "Wait! I'll soon stop that. Now, who else is there?"

"The marchese, sometimes, and the canons of the Collegiate Church."

"Married?"

"The canons——" he began with twinkling eyes.

"Oh, I forgot your horrid celibacy. In England they would be the centre of everything. But why shouldn't I know them? Would it make it easier if I called all round? Isn't that your foreign way?"

He did not think it would make it easier.

"But I must know some one! Who were the men you were talking to this afternoon?"

Low-class men. He could scarcely recollect their names.

"But, Gino dear, if they're low class, why did you talk to them? Don't you care about your position?"

All Gino cared about at present was idleness and pocket-money, and his way of expressing it was to exclaim, "Ouf—pouf! How hot it is in here. No air; I sweat all over. I expire. I must cool myself, or I shall never get to sleep." In his funny abrupt way he ran out on to the loggia, where he lay full length on the parapet, and began to smoke and spit under the silence of the stars.

Lilia gathered somehow from this conversation that Continental society was not the go-as-you-please thing she had expected. Indeed she could not see where Continental society was. Italy is such a delightful place to live in if you happen to be a man. There one may enjoy that exquisite luxury of Socialism—that true Socialism which is based not on equality of income or character, but on the equality of manners. In the democracy of the *caffè* or the street the great question of our life has been solved, and the brotherhood of man is a reality. But is accomplished at the expense of the sisterhood of women. Why should you not make friends with your neighbour at the theatre or in the train, when you know and he knows that feminine criticism and feminine insight and feminine prejudice will never come between you? Though you become as David and Jonathan, you need never enter his home, nor he yours. All your lives you will meet under the open air, the only rooftree of the South, under which he will spit and swear, and you will drop your h's, and nobody will think the worse of either.

Meanwhile the women—they have, of course, their house and their church, with its admirable and frequent services, to which they are escorted by the maid. Otherwise they do not go out much, for it is not genteel to walk, and you are too poor to keep a carriage. Occasionally you will take them to the *caffè* or theatre, and immediately all your wonted acquaintance there desert you, except those few who are expecting and expected to marry into your family. It is all very sad. But one consolation emerges—life is very pleasant in Italy if you are a man.

Hitherto Gino had not interfered with Lilia. She was so much older than he was, and so much richer, that he regarded her as a superior being who answered to other laws. He was not wholly surprised, for strange rumours were always blowing over the Alps of lands where men and women had the same amusements and interests, and he had often met that privileged maniac, the lady tourist, on her solitary walks. Lilia took solitary walks too, and only that week a tramp had grabbed at her watch—an episode which is supposed to be indigenous in Italy, though really less frequent there than in Bond Street. Now that he knew her better, he was inevitably losing his awe: no one could live with her and keep it, especially when she had been so silly as to lose a gold watch and chain. As he lay thoughtful along the parapet, he realized for the first time the responsibilities of married life. He must save her from dangers, physical and social, for after all she was a woman. "And I," he reflected, "though I am young, am at all events a man, and know what is right."

He found her still in the living-room, combing her hair, for she had something of the slattern in her nature, and there was no need to keep up appearances.

"You must not go out alone," he said gently. "It is not safe. If you want to walk, Perfetta shall accompany you." Perfetta was a widowed cousin, too humble for social aspirations, who was living with them as factotum.

"Very well," smiled Lilia, "very well"—as if she were addressing a solicitous kitten. But for all that she never took a solitary walk again, with one exception, till the day of her death.

Days passed, and no one called except poor relatives. She began to feel dull. Didn't he know the Sindaco or the bank manager? Even the landlady of the Stella d'Italia would be better than no one. She, when she went into the town, was pleasantly received; but people naturally found a difficulty in getting on with a lady who could not learn their language. And the tea-party, under Gino's adroit management, receded ever and ever before her.

He had a good deal of anxiety over her welfare, for she did not settle down in the house at all. But he was comforted by a welcome and unexpected visitor. As he was going one afternoon for the letters—they were delivered at the door, but it took longer to get them at the office—some one humorously threw a cloak over his head, and when he disengaged himself he saw his very dear friend Spiridione Tesi of the custom-house at Chiasso, whom he had not met for two years. What joy! what salutations! so that all the passers-by smiled with approval on the amiable scene. Spiridione's brother was now station-master at Bologna, and thus he himself could spend his holiday travelling over Italy at the public expense. Hearing of Gino's marriage, he had come to see him on his way to Siena, where lived his own uncle, lately married too.

"They all do it," he exclaimed, "myself excepted." He was not quite twenty-three. "But tell me more. She is English. That is good, very good. An English wife is very good indeed. And she is rich?"

"Immensely rich."

"Blonde or dark?"

"Blonde."

"Is it possible!"

"It pleases me very much," said Gino simply. "If you remember, I always desired a blonde." Three or four men had collected, and were listening.

"We all desire one," said Spiridione. "But you, Gino, deserve your good fortune, for you are a good son, a brave man, and a true friend, and from the very first moment I saw you I wished you well."

"No compliments, I beg," said Gino, standing

with his hands crossed on his chest and a smile of pleasure on his face.

Spiridione addressed the other men, none of whom he had ever seen before. "Is it not true? Does not he deserve this wealthy blonde?"

"He does deserve her," said all the men.

It is a marvellous land, where you love it or hate it.

There were no letters, and of course they sat down at the Caffè Garibaldi, by the Collegiate Church—quite a good *caffè* that for so small a city. There were marble-topped tables, and pillars terracotta below and gold above, and on the ceiling was a fresco of the battle of Solferino. One could not have desired a prettier room. They had vermouth and little cakes with sugar on the top, which they chose gravely at the counter, pinching them first to be sure they were fresh. And though vermouth is barely alcoholic, Spiridione drenched his with soda-water to be sure that it should not get into his head.

They were in high spirits, and elaborate compliments alternated curiously with gentle horseplay. But soon they put up their legs on a pair of chairs and began to smoke.

"Tell me," said Spiridione—"I forgot to ask—is she young?"

"Thirty-three."

"Ah, well, we cannot have everything."

"But you would be surprised. Had she told me twenty-eight, I should not have disbelieved her."

"Is she *simpatica*?" (Nothing will translate that word.)

Gino dabbed at the sugar and said after a silence, "Sufficiently so."

"It is a most important thing."

"She is rich, she is generous, she is affable, she addresses her inferiors without haughtiness."

There was another silence. "It is not sufficient," said the other. "One does not define it thus." He lowered his voice to a whisper. "Last month a German was smuggling cigars. The custom-house was dark. Yet I refused because I did not like him. The gifts of such men do not bring happiness. *Non era simpatico.* He paid for every one, and the fine for deception besides."

"Do you gain much beyond your pay?" asked Gino, diverted for an instant.

"I do not accept small sums now. It is not worth the risk. But the German was another matter. But listen, my Gino, for I am older than you and more full of experience. The person who understands us at first sight, who never irritates us, who never bores, to whom we can pour forth every thought and wish, not only in speech but in silence—that is what I mean by *simpatico.*"

"There are such men, I know," said Gino. "And I have heard it said of children. But where will you find such a woman?"

"That is true. Here you are wiser than I. *Sono poco simpatiche le donne.* And the time we waste over them is much." He sighed dolefully, as if he found the nobility of his sex a burden.

"One I have seen who may be so. She spoke very little, but she was a young lady—different to most. She, too, was English, the companion of my wife here. But Fra Filippo, the brother-in-law, took her back with him. I saw them start. He was very angry."

Then he spoke of his exciting and secret marriage, and they made fun of the unfortunate Philip, who had travelled over Europe to stop it.

"I regret though," said Gino, when they had finished laughing, "that I toppled him on to the bed. A great tall man! And when I am really amused I am often impolite."

"You will never see him again," said Spiridione, who carried plenty of philosophy about him. "And by now the scene will have passed from his mind."

"It sometimes happens that such things are recollected longest. I shall never see him again, of course; but it is no benefit to me that he should wish me ill. And even if he has forgotten, I am still sorry that I toppled him on to the bed."

So their talk continued, at one moment full of childishness and tender wisdom, the next moment scandalously gross. The shadows of the terra-cotta pillars lengthened, and tourists, flying through the Palazzo Pubblico opposite, could observe how the Italians wasted time.

The sight of tourists reminded Gino of something he might say. "I want to consult you since you are so kind as to take an interest in my affairs. My wife wishes to take solitary walks."

Spiridione was shocked.

"But I have forbidden her."

"Naturally."

"She does not yet understand. She asked me to

accompany her sometimes—to walk without object! You know, she would like me to be with her all day."

"I see, I see." He knitted his brows and tried to think how he could help his friend. "She needs employment. Is she a Catholic?"

"No."

"That is a pity. She must be persuaded. It will be a great solace to her when she is alone."

"I am a Catholic, but of course I never go to church."

"Of course not. Still, you might take her at first. That is what my brother has done with his wife at Bologna and he has joined the Free Thinkers. He took her once or twice himself, and now she has acquired the habit and continues to go without him."

"Most excellent advice, and I thank you for it. But she wishes to give tea-parties—men and women together whom she has never seen."

"Oh, the English! they are always thinking of tea. They carry it by the kilogramme in their trunks, and they are so clumsy that they always pack it at the top. But it is absurd!"

"What am I to do about it?"

"Do nothing. Or ask me!"

"Come!" cried Gino, springing up. "She will be quite pleased."

The dashing young fellow coloured crimson. "Of course I was only joking."

"I know. But she wants me to take my friends. Come now! Waiter!"

"If I do come," cried the other, "and take tea with you, this bill must be my affair."

"Certainly not; you are in my country!"

A long argument ensued, in which the waiter took part, suggesting various solutions. At last Gino triumphed. The bill came to eightpence-halfpenny, and a halfpenny for the waiter brought it up to ninepence. Then there was a shower of gratitude on one side and of deprecation on the other, and when courtesies were at their height they suddenly linked arms and swung down the street, tickling each other with lemonade straws as they went.

Lilia was delighted to see them, and became more animated than Gino had known her for a long time. The tea tasted of chopped hay, and they asked to be allowed to drink it out of a wine-glass, and refused milk; but, as she repeatedly observed, this was something like. Spiridione's manners were very agreeable. He kissed her hand on introduction, and as his profession had taught him a little English, conversation did not flag.

"Do you like music?" she asked.

"Passionately," he replied. "I have not studied scientific music, but the music of the heart, yes."

So she played on the humming piano very badly, and he sang, not so badly. Gino got out a guitar and sang too, sitting out on the loggia. It was a most agreeable visit.

Gino said he would just walk his friend back to his lodgings. As they went he said, without the least trace of malice or satire in his voice, "I think you are quite right. I shall not bring people to the house any more. I do not see why an English wife should be treated differently. This is Italy."

"You are very wise," exclaimed the other; "very

wise indeed. The more precious a possession the more carefully it should be guarded."

They had reached the lodging, but went on as far as the Caffè Garibaldi, where they spent a long and most delightful evening.

Chapter Four

THE ADVANCE OF regret can be so gradual that it is impossible to say "yesterday I was happy, today I am not." At no one moment did Lilia realize that her marriage was a failure; yet during the summer and autumn she became as unhappy as it was possible for her nature to be. She had no unkind treatment, and few unkind words, from her husband. He simply left her alone. In the morning he went out to do "business," which, as far as she could discover, meant sitting in the Farmacia. He usually returned to lunch, after which he retired to another room and slept. In the evening he grew vigorous again, and took the air on the ramparts, often having his dinner out, and seldom returning till midnight or later. There were, of course, the times when he was away altogether—at Empoli, Siena, Florence, Bologna—for he delighted in travel, and seemed to pick up friends all over the country. Lilia often heard what a favourite he was.

She began to see that she must assert herself, but she could not see how. Her self-confidence, which had overthrown Philip, had gradually oozed away. If she left the strange house there was the strange little town. If she were to disobey her husband and walk in the country, that would be stranger still—vast slopes of olives and vineyards, with chalk-white farms, and in the distance other slopes, with more olives and more farms, and more little towns outlined against the cloudless sky. "I don't call this country," she would say. "Why, it's not as wild as Sawston Park!" And, indeed, there was scarcely a touch of wildness in it—some of those slopes had been under cultivation for two thousand years. But it was terrible and mysterious all the same, and its continued presence made Lilia so uncomfortable that she forgot her nature and began to reflect.

She reflected chiefly about her marriage. The ceremony had been hasty and expensive, and the rites, whatever they were, were not those of the Church of England. Lilia had no religion in her; but for hours at a time she would be seized with a vulgar fear that she was not "married properly," and that her social position in the next world might be as obscure as it was in this. It might be safer to do the thing thoroughly, and one day she took the advice of Spiridione and joined the Roman Catholic Church, or as she called it, "Santa Deodata's." Gino approved; he, too, thought it safer, and it was fun confessing, though the priest was a stupid old man, and the whole thing was a good slap in the face for the people at home.

The people at home took the slap very soberly; indeed, there were few left for her to give it to. The Herritons were out of the question; they would not even let her write to Irma, though Irma was occasionally allowed to write to her. Mrs. Theobald was rapidly subsiding into dotage, and, as far as she could be definite about anything, had definitely sided with the Herritons. And Miss Abbott did likewise. Night after night did Lilia curse this false friend, who had agreed with her that the marriage would "do," and that the Herritons would come round to it, and then, at the first hint of opposition, had fled back to England shrieking and distraught. Miss Abbott headed the long list of those who should never be written to, and who should never be forgiven. Almost the only person who was not on that list was Mr. Kingcroft, who had unexpectedly sent an affectionate and inquiring letter. He was quite sure never to cross the Channel, and Lilia drew freely on her fancy in the reply.

At first she had seen a few English people, for Monteriano was not the end of the earth. One or two inquisitive ladies, who had heard at home of her quarrel with the Herritons, came to call. She was very sprightly, and they thought her quite unconventional, and Gino a charming boy, so all that was to the good. But by May the season, such as it was, had finished, and there would be no one till next spring. As Mrs. Herriton had often observed, Lilia had no resources. She did not like music, or reading, or work. Her one qualification for life was rather blowsy high spirits, which turned querulous or boisterous according to circumstances. She was not obedient, but she was cowardly, and in the most gentle way, which Mrs. Herriton might have envied, Gino made her do what he wanted. At first it had been rather fun to let him get the upper hand. But it was galling to discover that he could not do otherwise. He had a good strong will when he chose to use it, and would not have had the least scruple in using bolts and locks to put it into effect. There was plenty of brutality deep down in him, and one day Lilia nearly touched it.

It was the old question of going out alone.

"I always do it in England."

"This is Italy."

"Yes, but I'm older than you, and I'll settle."

"I am your husband," he said, smiling. They had finished their mid-day meal, and he wanted to go and sleep. Nothing would rouse him up, until at last Lilia, getting more and more angry, said, "And I've got the money."

He looked horrified.

Now was the moment to assert herself. She made the statement again. He got up from his chair.

"And you'd better mend your manners," she continued, "for you'd find it awkward if I stopped drawing cheques."

She was no reader of character, but she quickly became alarmed. As she said to Perfetta afterwards, "None of his clothes seemed to fit—too big in one place, too small in another." His figure rather than his face altered, the shoulders falling forward till his coat wrinkled across his back and pulled away from his wrists. He seemed all arms. He edged round the table to where she was sitting, and she sprang away and held the chair between them, too frightened to speak or to move. He looked at her with round, expressionless eyes, and slowly stretched out his left hand.

Perfetta was heard coming up from the kitchen. It seemed to wake him up, and he turned away and went to his room without a word.

"What has happened?" cried Lilia, nearly fainting. "He is ill—ill."

Perfetta looked suspicious when she heard the account. "What did you say to him?" She crossed herself.

"Hardly anything," said Lilia and crossed herself also. Thus did the two women pay homage to their outraged male.

It was clear to Lilia at last that Gino had married her for money. But he had frightened her too much to leave any place for contempt. His return was terrifying, for he was frightened too, imploring her pardon, lying at her feet, embracing her, murmuring "It was not I," striving to define things which he did not understand. He stopped in the house for three days, positively ill with physical collapse. But for all his suffering he had tamed her, and she never threatened to cut off supplies again.

Perhaps he kept her even closer than convention demanded. But he was very young, and he could not bear it to be said of him that he did not know how to treat a lady—or to manage a wife. And his own social position was uncertain. Even in England a dentist is a troublesome creature, whom careful people find difficult to class. He hovers between the professions and the trades; he may be only a little lower than the doctors, or he may be down among the chemists, or even beneath them. The son of the Italian dentist felt this too. For himself nothing mattered; he made friends with the people he liked, for he was that glorious invariable creature, a man. But his wife should visit nowhere rather than visit wrongly: seclusion was both decent and safe. The social ideals of North and South had had their brief contention, and this time the South had won.

It would have been well if he had been as strict over his own behaviour as he was over hers. But the incongruity never occurred to him for a moment. His morality was that of the average Latin, and as he was suddenly placed in the position of a gentleman, he did not see why he should not behave as such. Of course, had Lilia been different—had she asserted herself and got a grip on his character—he might possibly—though not probably—have been made a better husband as well as a better man, and at all events he could have adopted the attitude of the Englishman, whose standard is higher even when his practice is the same. But had Lilia been different she might not have married him.

The discovery of his infidelity—which she made by accident—destroyed such remnants of self-satisfaction as her life might yet possess. She broke down utterly and sobbed and cried in Perfetta's arms. Perfetta was kind and even sympathetic, but cautioned her on no account to speak to Gino, who would be furious if he was suspected. And Lilia agreed, partly because she was afraid of him, partly because it was, after all, the best and most dignified thing to do. She had given up everything for him— her daughter, her relatives, her friends, all the little comforts and luxuries of a civilized life—and even if she had the courage to break away, there was no one who would receive her now. The Herritons had been almost malignant in their efforts against her, and all her friends had one by one fallen off. So it was better to live on humbly, trying not to feel, endeavouring by a cheerful demeanour to put things right. "Perhaps," she thought, "if I have a child he will be different. I know he wants a son."

Lilia had achieved pathos despite herself, for there are some situations in which vulgarity counts no longer. Not Cordelia nor Imogen more deserves our tears.

She herself cried frequently, making herself look plain and old, which distressed her husband. He was particularly kind to her when he hardly ever saw her, and she accepted his kindness without resentment, even with gratitude, so docile had she become. She did not hate him, even as she had never loved him; with her it was only when she was excited that the semblance of either passion arose. People said she was headstrong, but really her weak brain left her cold.

Suffering, however, is more independent of temperament, and the wisest of women could hardly have suffered more.

As for Gino, he was quite as boyish as ever, and carried his iniquities like a feather. A favourite speech of his was, "Ah, one ought to marry! Spiridione is wrong; I must persuade him. Not till marriage does one realize the pleasures and the possibilities of life." So saying, he would take down his felt hat, strike it in the right place as infallibly as a German strikes his in the wrong place, and leave her.

One evening, when he had gone out thus, Lilia could stand it no longer. It was September. Sawston would be just filling up after the summer holidays. People would be running in and out of each other's houses all along the road. There were bicycle gymkhanas, and on the 30th Mrs. Herriton would be holding the annual bazaar in her garden for the C.M.S. It seemed impossible that such a free, happy life could exist. She walked out on to the loggia. Moonlight and stars in a soft purple sky. The walls of Monteriano should be glorious on such a night as this. But the house faced away from them.

Perfetta was banging in the kitchen, and the stairs down led past the kitchen door. But the stairs up to the attic—the stairs no one ever used—opened out of the living-room, and by unlocking the door at the top one might slip out on to the square terrace above the house, and thus for ten minutes walk in freedom and peace.

The key was in the pocket of Gino's best suit—the English check—which he never wore. The stairs creaked and the key-hole screamed; but Perfetta was growing deaf. The walls were beautiful, but as they faced west they were in shadow. To see the light upon them she must walk round the town a little, till they were caught by the beams of the rising moon. She looked anxiously at the house, and started.

It was easy walking, for a little path ran all outside the ramparts. The few people she met wished her a civil good-night, taking her, in her hatless condition, for a peasant. The walls trended round towards the moon; and presently she came into its light, and saw all the rough towers turn into pillars of silver and black, and the ramparts into cliffs of pearl. She had no great sense of beauty, but she was sentimental, and she began to cry; for here, where a great cypress interrupted the monotony of the girdle of olives, she had sat with Gino one afternoon in March, her head upon his shoulder, while Caroline was looking at the view and sketching. Round the corner was the Siena gate, from which the road to England started, and she could hear the rumble of the diligence which was going down to catch the night train to Empoli. The next moment it was upon her, for the highroad came towards her a little before it began its long zigzag down the hill.

The driver slackened, and called to her to get in. He did not know who she was. He hoped she might be coming to the station.

"Non vengo!" she cried.

He wished her good-night, and turned his horses down the corner. As the diligence came round she saw that it was empty.

"Vengo . . ."

Her voice was tremulous, and did not carry. The horses swung off.

"Vengo! Vengo!"

He had begun to sing, and heard nothing. She ran down the road screaming to him to stop—that she was coming; while the distance grew greater and the noise of the diligence increased. The man's back was black and square against the moon, and if he would but turn for an instant she would be saved.

She tried to cut off the corner of the zigzag, stumbling over the great clods of earth, large and hard as rocks, which lay between the eternal olives. She was too late; for, just before she regained the road, the thing swept past her, thunderous, ploughing up choking clouds of moonlit dust.

She did not call any more, for she felt very ill, and fainted; and when she revived she was lying in the road, with dust in her eyes, and dust in her mouth, and dust down her ears. There is something very terrible in dust at night-time.

"What shall I do?" she moaned. "He will be so angry."

And without further effort she slowly climbed back to captivity, shaking her garments as she went.

Ill luck pursued her to the end. It was one of the nights when Gino happened to come in. He was in the kitchen, swearing and smashing plates, while Perfetta, her apron over her head, was weeping violently. At the sight of Lilia he turned upon her and poured forth a flood of miscellaneous abuse. He was far more angry but much less alarming than he had been that day when he edged after her round the table. And Lilia gained more courage from her bad conscience than she ever had from her good one, for as he spoke she was seized with indignation and feared him no longer, and saw him for a cruel, worthless, hypocritical, dissolute upstart, and spoke in return.

Perfetta screamed for she told him everything— all she knew and all she thought. He stood with open mouth, all the anger gone out of him, feeling ashamed, and an utter fool. He was fairly and right-

fully cornered. When had husband so given himself
away before? She finished; and he was dumb, for she
had spoken truly. Then, alas! the absurdity of his
own position grew upon him, and he laughed—as he
would have laughed at the same situation on the
stage.

"You laugh?" stammered Lilia.

"Ah!" he cried, "who could help it? I, who
thought you knew and saw nothing—I am tricked—I
am conquered. I give in. Let us talk of it no more."

He touched her on the shoulder like a good
comrade, half amused and half penitent, and then,
murmuring and smiling to himself, ran quietly out of
the room.

Perfetta burst into congratulations. "What courage you have!" she cried; "and what good fortune! He
is angry no longer! He has forgiven you!"

Neither Perfetta, nor Gino, nor Lilia herself knew
the true reason of all the misery that followed. To the
end he thought that kindness and a little attention
would be enough to set things straight. His wife was
a very ordinary woman, and why should her ideas
differ from his own? No one realized that more than
personalities were engaged; that the struggle was na-
tional; that generations of ancestors, good, bad, or indifferent, forbad the Latin man to be chivalrous to
the northern woman, the northern woman to forgive
the Latin man. All this might have been foreseen:
Mrs. Herriton foresaw it from the first.

Meanwhile Lilia prided herself on her high personal standard, and Gino simply wondered why she
did not come round. He hated discomfort and
yearned for sympathy, but shrank from mentioning

his difficulties in the town in case they were put down to his own incompetence. Spiridione was told, and replied in a philosophical but not very helpful letter. His other great friend, whom he trusted more, was still serving in Eritrea or some other desolate outpost. It would take too long to explain everything to him. And, besides, what was the good of letters? Friends cannot travel through the post.

Lilia, so similar to her husband in many ways, yearned for comfort and sympathy too. The night he laughed at her she wildly took up paper and pen and wrote page after page, analysing his character, enumerating his iniquities, reporting whole conversations, tracing all the causes and the growth of her misery. She was beside herself with passion, and though she could hardly think or see, she suddenly attained to magnificence and pathos which a practised stylist might have envied. It was written like a diary, and not till its conclusion did she realize for whom it was meant.

"Irma, darling Irma, this letter is for you. I almost forgot I have a daughter. It will make you unhappy, but I want you to know everything, and you cannot learn things too soon. God bless you, my dearest, and save you. God bless your miserable mother."

Fortunately Mrs. Herriton was in when the letter arrived. She seized it and opened it in her bedroom. Another moment, and Irma's placid childhood would have been destroyed for ever.

Lilia received a brief note from Harriet, again forbidding direct communication between mother and daughter, and concluding with formal condolences. It nearly drove her mad.

"Gently! gently!" said her husband. They were sitting together on the loggia when the letter arrived. He often sat with her now, watching her for hours, puzzled and anxious, but not contrite.

"It's nothing." She went in and tore it up, and then began to write—a very short letter, whose gist was "Come and save me."

It is not good to see your wife crying when she writes—especially if you are conscious that, on the whole, your treatment of her has been reasonable and kind. It is not good, when you accidentally look over her shoulder, to see that she is writing to a man. Nor should she shake her fist at you when she leaves the room, under the impression that you are engaged in lighting a cigar and cannot see her.

Lilia went to the post herself. But in Italy so many things can be arranged. The postman was a friend of Gino's, and Mr. Kingcroft never got his letter.

So she gave up hope, became ill, and all through the autumn lay in bed. Gino was distracted. She knew why; he wanted a son. He could talk and think of nothing else. His one desire was to become the father of a man like himself, and it held him with a grip he only partially understood, for it was the first great desire, the first great passion of his life. Falling in love was a mere physical triviality, like warm sun or cool water, beside this divine hope of immortality: "I continue." He gave candles to Santa Deodata, for he was always religious at a crisis, and sometimes he went to her himself and prayed the crude uncouth demands of the simple. Impetuously he summoned all his relatives back to bear him company in his time of need, and Lilia saw strange faces flitting past her in the darkened room.

"My love!" he would say, "my dearest Lilia! Be calm. I have never loved any one but you."

She, knowing everything, would only smile gently, too broken by suffering to make sarcastic repartees.

Before the child was born he gave her a kiss, and said, "I have prayed all night for a boy."

Some strangely tender impulse moved her, and she said faintly, "You are a boy yourself, Gino."

He answered, "Then we shall be brothers."

He lay outside the room with his head against the door like a dog. When they came to tell him the glad news they found him half unconscious, and his face was wet with tears.

As for Lilia, some one said to her, "It is a beautiful boy!" But she had died in giving birth to him.

Chapter Five

AT THE TIME of Lilia's death Philip Herriton was just
twenty-four years of age—indeed the news reached
Sawston on his birthday. He was a tall, weakly-built
young man, whose clothes had to be judiciously padded on the shoulders in order to make him pass
muster. His face was plain rather than not, and there
was a curious mixture in it of good and bad. He had
a fine forehead and a good large nose, and both ob-
servation and sympathy were in his eyes. But below
the nose and eyes all was confusion, and those
people who believe that destiny resides in the mouth
and chin shook their heads when they looked at him.

Philip himself, as a boy, had been keenly conscious of these defects. Sometimes when he had been
bullied or hustled about at school he would retire to
his cubicle and examine his features in a looking-
glass, and he would sigh and say, "It is a weak face.

I shall never carve a place for myself in the world."
But as years went on he became either less self-
conscious or more self-satisfied. The world, he
found, made a niche for him as it did for every one.
Decision of character might come later—or he might
have it without knowing. At all events he had got a
sense of beauty and a sense of humour, two most de-
sirable gifts. The sense of beauty developed first. It
caused him at the age of twenty to wear parti-
coloured ties and a squashy hat, to be late for dinner
on account of the sunset, and to catch art from
Burne-Jones to Praxiteles. At twenty-two he went to
Italy with some cousins, and there he absorbed into
one æsthetic whole olive-trees, blue sky, frescoes,
country inns, saints, peasants, mosaics, statues, beggars. He came back with the air of a prophet who
would either remodel Sawston or reject it. All the en-
ergies and enthusiasms of a rather friendless life had
passed into the championship of beauty.

In a short time it was over. Nothing had happened either in Sawston or within himself. He had
shocked half-a-dozen people, squabbled with his sister, and bickered with his mother. He concluded that
nothing could happen, not knowing that human love
and love of truth sometimes conquer where love of
beauty fails.

A little disenchanted, a little tired, but æstheti-cal-
ly intact, he resumed his placid life, relying more and
more on his second gift, the gift of humour. If he
could not reform the world, he could at all events
laugh at it, thus attaining at least an intellectual supe-
riority. Laughter, he read and believed, was a sign of
good moral health, and he laughed on contentedly,

till Lilia's marriage toppled contentment down for ever. Italy, the land of beauty, was ruined for him. She had no power to change men and things who dwelt in her. She, too, could produce avarice, brutality, stupidity—and, what was worse, vulgarity. It was on her soil and through her influence that a silly woman had married a cad. He hated Gino, the betrayer of his life's ideal, and now that the sordid tragedy had come, it filled him with pangs, not of sympathy, but of final disillusion.

The disillusion was convenient for Mrs. Herriton, who saw a trying little period ahead of her, and was glad to have her family united.

"Are we to go into mourning, do you think?" She always asked her children's advice where possible.

Harriet thought that they should. She had been detestable to Lilia while she lived, but she always felt that the dead deserve attention and sympathy. "After all she has suffered. That letter kept me awake for nights. The whole thing is like one of those horrible modern plays where no one is in the right. But if we have mourning, it will mean telling Irma."

"Of course we must tell Irma!" said Philip.

"Of course," said his mother. "But I think we can still not tell her about Lilia's marriage."

"I don't think that. And she must have suspected something by now."

"So one would have supposed. But she never cared for her mother, and little girls of nine don't reason clearly. She looks on it as a long visit. And it is important, most important, that she should not receive a shock. All a child's life depends on the ideal it has of its parents. Destroy that and everything goes—morals, behaviour, everything. Absolute trust in some one else is the essence of education. That is why I have been so careful about talking of poor Lilia before her."

"But you forget this wretched baby. Waters and Adamson write that there is a baby."

"Mrs. Theobald must be told. But she doesn't count. She is breaking up very quickly. She doesn't even see Mr. Kingcroft now. He, thank goodness, I hear, has at last consoled himself with someone else."

"The child must know some time," persisted Philip, who felt a little displeased, though he could not tell with what.

"The later the better. Every moment she is developing."

"I must say it seems rather hard luck, doesn't it?"

"On Irma? Why?"

"On us, perhaps. We have morals and behaviour also, and I don't think this continual secrecy improves them."

"There's no need to twist the thing round to that," said Harriet, rather disturbed.

"Of course there isn't," said her mother. "Let's keep to the main issue. This baby's quite beside the point. Mrs. Theobald will do nothing, and it's no concern of ours."

"It will make a difference in the money, surely," said he.

"No, dear; very little. Poor Charles provided for every kind of contingency in his will. The money will come to you and Harriet, as Irma's guardians."

"Good. Does the Italian get anything?"

"He will get all hers. But you know what that is."

"Good. So those are our tactics—to tell no one about the baby, not even Miss Abbott."

"Most certainly this is the proper course," said Mrs. Herriton, preferring "course" to "tactics" for Harriet's sake. "And why ever should we tell Caroline?"

"She was so mixed up in the affair."

"Poor silly creature. The less she hears about it the better she will be pleased. I have come to be very sorry for Caroline. She, if any one, has suffered and been penitent. She burst into tears when I told her a little, only a little, of that terrible letter. I never saw such genuine remorse. We must forgive her and forget. Let the dead bury their dead. We will not trouble her with them."

Philip saw that his mother was scarcely logical. But there was no advantage in saying so. "Here beginneth the New Life, then. Do you remember, mother, that was what we said when we saw Lilia off?"

"Yes, dear; but now it is really a New Life, because we are all at accord. Then you were still infatuated with Italy. It may be full of beautiful pictures and churches, but we cannot judge a country by anything but its men."

"That is quite true," he said sadly. And as the tactics were now settled, he went out and took an aimless and solitary walk.

By the time he came back two important things had happened. Irma had been told of her mother's death, and Miss Abbott, who had called for a subscription, had been told also.

Irma had wept loudly, had asked a few sensible

questions and a good many silly ones, and had been content with evasive answers. Fortunately the school prize-giving was at hand, and that, together with the prospect of new black clothes, kept her from meditating on the fact that Lilia, who had been absent so long, would now be absent for ever.

"As for Caroline," said Mrs. Herriton, "I was almost frightened. She broke down utterly. She cried even when she left the house. I comforted her as best I could, and I kissed her. It is something that the breach between her and ourselves is now entirely healed."

"Did she ask no questions—as to the nature of Lilia's death, I mean?"

"She did. But she has a mind of extraordinary delicacy. She saw that I was reticent, and she did not press me. You see, Philip, I can say to you what I could not say before Harriet. Her ideas are so crude. Really we do not want it known in Sawston that there is a baby. All peace and comfort would be lost if people came inquiring after it."

His mother knew how to manage him. He agreed enthusiastically. And a few days later, when he chanced to travel up to London with Miss Abbott, he had all the time the pleasant thrill of one who is better informed. Their last journey together had been from Monteriano back across Europe. It had been a ghastly journey, and Philip, from the force of association, rather expected something ghastly now.

He was surprised. Miss Abbott, between Sawston and Charing Cross, revealed qualities which he had never guessed her to possess. Without being exactly original, she did show a commendable intelligence, and though at times she was gauche and even un-courtly, he felt that here was a person whom it might be well to cultivate.

At first she annoyed him. They were talking, of course, about Lilia, when she broke the thread of vague commiseration and said abruptly, "It is all so strange as well as so tragic. And what I did was as strange as anything."

It was the first reference she had ever made to her contemptible behaviour. "Never mind," he said. "It's all over now. Let the dead bury their dead. It's fallen out of our lives."

"But that's why I can talk about it and tell you everything I have always wanted to. You thought me stupid and sentimental and wicked and mad, but you never really knew how much I was to blame."

"Indeed I never think about it now," said Philip gently. He knew that her nature was in the main gen-erous and upright: it was unnecessary for her to reveal her thoughts.

"The first evening we got to Monteriano," she persisted, "Lilia went out for a walk alone, saw that Italian in a picturesque position on a wall, and fell in love. He was shabbily dressed, and she did not even know he was the son of a dentist. I must tell you I was used to this sort of thing. Once or twice before I had had to send people about their business."

"Yes; we counted on you," said Philip, with sud-den sharpness. After all, if she would reveal her thoughts, she must take the consequences.

"I know you did," she retorted with equal sharp-ness. "Lilia saw him several times again, and I knew I ought to interfere. I called her to my bedroom one night. She was very frightened, for she knew what it was about and how severe I could be. 'Do you love this man?' I asked. 'Yes or no?' She said 'Yes.' And I said, 'Why don't you marry him if you think you'll be happy?' "

"Really—really," exploded Philip, as exasperated as if the thing had happened yesterday. "You knew Lilia all your life. Apart from everything else—as if she could choose what could make her happy!"

"Had you ever let her choose?" she flashed out. "I'm afraid that's rude," she added, trying to calm herself.

"Let us rather say unhappily expressed," said Philip, who always adopted a dry satirical manner when he was puzzled.

"I want to finish. Next morning I found Signor Carella and said the same to him. He—well, he was willing. That's all."

"And the telegram?" He looked scornfully out of the window.

Hitherto her voice had been hard, possibly in self-accusation, possibly in defiance. Now it became unmistakably sad. "Ah, the telegram! That was wrong. Lilia there was more cowardly than I was. We should have told the truth. It lost me my nerve, at all events. I came to the station meaning to tell you everything then. But we had started with a lie, and I got frightened. And at the end, when you left, I got frightened again and came with you."

"Did you really mean to stop?"

"For a time, at all events."

"Would that have suited a newly married pair?"

"It would have suited them. Lilia needed me.

And as for him—I can't help feeling I might have got influence over him."

"I am ignorant of these matters," said Philip; "but I should have thought that would have increased the difficulty of the situation."

The crisp remark was wasted on her. She looked hopelessly at the raw over-built country, and said, "Well, I have explained."

"But pardon me, Miss Abbott; of most of your conduct you have given a description rather than an explanation."

He had fairly caught her, and expected that she would gape and collapse. To his surprise she answered with some spirit, "An explanation may bore you, Mr. Herriton: it drags in other topics."

"Oh, never mind."

"I hated Sawston, you see."

He was delighted. "So did and do I. That's splendid. Go on."

"I hated the idleness, the stupidity, the respectability, the petty unselfishness."

"Petty selfishness," he corrected. Sawston psychology had long been his specialty.

"Petty unselfishness," she repeated. "I had got an idea that every one here spent their lives in making little sacrifices for objects they didn't care for, to please people they didn't love; that they never learnt to be sincere—and, what's as bad, never learnt how to enjoy themselves. That's what I thought—what I thought at Monteriano."

"Why, Miss Abbott," he cried, "you should have told me this before! Think it still! I agree with lots of it. Magnificent!"

"Now Lilia," she went on, "though there were things about her I didn't like, had somehow kept the power of enjoying herself with sincerity. And Gino, I thought, was splendid, and young, and strong not only in body, and sincere as the day. If they wanted to marry, why shouldn't they do so? Why shouldn't she break with the deadening life where she had got into a groove, and would go on in it, getting more and more—worse than unhappy—apathetic till she died? Of course I was wrong. She only changed one groove for another—a worse groove. And as for him—well, you know more about him than I do. I can never trust myself to judge characters again. But I still feel he cannot have been quite bad when we first met him. Lilia—that I should dare to say it!—must have been cowardly. He was only a boy—just going to turn into something fine, I thought—and she must have mismanaged him. So that is the one time I have gone against what is proper, and there are the results. You have an explanation now."

"And much of it has been most interesting, though I don't understand everything. Did you never think of the disparity of their social position?"

"We were mad—drunk with rebellion. We had no common-sense. As soon as you came, you saw and foresaw everything."

"Oh, I don't think that." He was vaguely displeased at being credited with common-sense. For a moment Miss Abbott had seemed to him more unconventional than himself.

"I hope you see," she concluded, "why I have troubled you with this long story. Women—I heard you say the other day—are never at ease till they tell their faults out loud. Lilia is dead and her husband gone to the bad—all through me. You see, Mr. Herriton, it makes me specially unhappy; it's the only time I've ever gone into what my father calls 'real life'—and look what I've made of it! All that winter I seemed to be waking up to beauty and splendour and I don't know what; and when the spring came, I wanted to fight against the things I hated— mediocrity and dulness and spitefulness and society. I actually hated society for a day or two at Monteriano. I didn't see that all these things are invincible, and that if we go against them they will break us to pieces. Thank you for listening to so much nonsense."

"Oh, I quite sympathize with what you say," said Philip encouragingly; "it isn't nonsense, and a year or two ago I should have been saying it too. But I feel differently now, and I hope that you also will change. Society is invincible—to a certain degree. But your real life is your own, and nothing can touch it. There is no power on earth that can prevent your criticizing and despising mediocrity—nothing that can stop you retreating into splendour and beauty—into the thoughts and beliefs that make the real life—the real you."

"I have never had that experience yet. Surely I and my life must be where I live."

Evidently she had the usual feminine incapacity for grasping philosophy. But she had developed quite a personality, and he must see more of her. "There is another great consolation against invincible mediocrity," he said—"the meeting a fellow-victim. I hope that this is only the first of many discussions that we shall have together."

She made a suitable reply. The train reached Charing Cross, and they parted,—he to go to a matinée, she to buy petticoats for the corpulent poor. Her thoughts wandered as she bought them: the gulf between herself and Mr. Herriton, which she had always known to be great, now seemed to her immeasurable.

These events and conversations took place at Christmas-time. The New Life initiated by them lasted some seven months. Then a little incident—a mere little vexatious incident—brought it to its close.

Irma collected picture post-cards, and Mrs. Herriton or Harriet always glanced first at all that came, lest the child should get hold of something vulgar. On this occasion the subject seemed perfectly inoffensive—a lot of ruined factory chimneys—and Harriet was about to hand it to her niece when her eye was caught by the words on the margin. She gave a shriek and flung the card into the grate. Of course no fire was alight in July, and Irma only had to run and pick it out again.

"How dare you!" screamed her aunt. "You wicked girl! Give it here!"

Unfortunately Mrs. Herriton was out of the room. Irma, who was not in awe of Harriet, danced round the table, reading as she did so, "View of the superb city of Monteriano—from your lital brother."

Stupid Harriet caught her, boxed her ears, and tore the post-card into fragments. Irma howled with pain, and began shouting indignantly, "Who is my little brother? Why have I never heard of him before?

Grandmamma! Grandmamma! Who is my little brother? Who is my——"

Mrs. Herriton swept into the room, saying, "Come with me, dear, and I will tell you. Now it is time for you to know."

Irma returned from the interview sobbing, though, as a matter of fact, she had learnt very little. But that little took hold of her imagination. She had promised secrecy—she knew not why. But what harm in talking of the little brother to those who had heard of him already?

"Aunt Harriet!" she would say. "Uncle Phil! Grandmamma! What do you suppose my little brother is doing now? Has he begun to play? Do Italian babies talk sooner than us, or would he be an English baby born abroad? Oh, I do long to see him, and be the first to teach him the Ten Commandments and the Catechism."

The last remark always made Harriet look grave.

"Really," exclaimed Mrs. Herriton, "Irma is getting too tiresome. She forgot poor Lilia soon enough."

"A living brother is more to her than a dead mother," said Philip dreamily. "She can knit him socks."

"I stopped that. She is bringing him in everywhere. It is most vexatious. The other night she asked if she might include him in the people she mentions specially in her prayers."

"What did you say?"

"Of course I allowed her," she replied coldly. "She has a right to mention any one she chooses. But

I was annoyed with her this morning, and I fear that I showed it."

"And what happened this morning?"

"She asked if she could pray for her 'new father'—for the Italian!"

"Did you let her?"

"I got up without saying anything."

"You must have felt just as you did when I wanted to pray for the devil."

"He is the devil," cried Harriet.

"No, Harriet; he is too vulgar."

"I will thank you not to scoff against religion!" was Harriet's retort. "Think of that poor baby. Irma is right to pray for him. What an entrance into life for an English child!"

"My dear sister, I can reassure you. Firstly, the beastly baby is Italian. Secondly, it was promptly christened at Santa Deodata's, and a powerful combination of saints watch over——"

"Don't, dear. And, Harriet, don't be so serious—I mean not so serious when you are with Irma. She will be worse than ever if she thinks we have something to hide."

Harriet's conscience could be quite as tiresome as Philip's unconventionality. Mrs. Herriton soon made it easy for her daughter to go for six weeks to the Tirol. Then she and Philip began to grapple with Irma alone.

Just as they had got things a little quiet the beastly baby sent another picture post-card—a comic one, not particularly proper. Irma received it while they were out, and all the trouble began again.

"I cannot think," said Mrs. Herriton, "what his motive is in sending them."

Two years before, Philip would have said that the motive was to give pleasure. Now he, like his mother, tried to think of something sinister and subtle.

"Do you suppose that he guesses the situation—how anxious we are to hush the scandal up?"

"That is quite possible. He knows that Irma will worry us about the baby. Perhaps he hopes that we shall adopt it to quiet her."

"Hopeful indeed."

"At the same time he has the chance of corrupting the child's morals." She unlocked a drawer, took out the post-card, and regarded it gravely. "He entreats her to send the baby one," was her next remark.

"She might do it too!"

"I told her not to; but we must watch her carefully, without, of course, appearing to be suspicious."

Philip was getting to enjoy his mother's diplomacy. He did not think of his own morals and behaviour any more.

"Who's to watch her at school, though? She may bubble out any moment."

"We can but trust to our influence," said Mrs. Herriton.

Irma did bubble out, that very day. She was proof against a single post-card, not against two. A new little brother is a valuable sentimental asset to a school-girl, and her school was then passing through an acute phase of baby-worship. Happy the girl who had her quiver full of them, who kissed them when she left home in the morning, who had the right to extricate them from mail-carts in the interval, who dangled them at tea ere they retired to rest! That one might sing the unwritten song of Miriam, blessed above all school-girls, who was allowed to hide her baby brother in a squashy place, where none but herself could find him!

How could Irma keep silent when pretentious girls spoke of baby cousins and baby visitors—she who had a baby brother, who wrote her post-cards through his dear papa? She had promised not to tell about him—she knew not why—and she told. And one girl told another, and one girl told her mother, and the thing was out.

"Yes, it is all very sad," Mrs. Herriton kept saying. "My daughter-in-law made a very unhappy marriage, as I dare say you know. I suppose that the child will be educated in Italy. Possibly his grandmother may be doing something, but I have not heard of it. I do not expect that she will have him over. She disapproves of the father. It is altogether a painful business for her."

She was careful only to scold Irma for disobedience—that eighth deadly sin, so convenient to parents and guardians. Harriet would have plunged into needless explanations and abuse. The child was ashamed, and talked about the baby less. The end of the school year was at hand, and she hoped to get another prize. But she also had put her hand to the wheel.

It was several days before they saw Miss Abbott. Mrs. Herriton had not come across her much since the kiss of reconciliation, nor Philip since the journey to London. She had, indeed, been rather a disap-

pointment to him. Her creditable display of original-
ity had never been repeated: he feared she was slip-
ping back. Now she came about the Cottage
Hospital—her life was devoted to dull acts of
charity—and though she got money out of him and
out of his mother, she still sat tight in her chair, looking graver and more wooden than ever.

"I dare say you have heard," said Mrs. Herriton,
well knowing what the matter was.

"Yes, I have. I came to ask you; have any steps
been taken?"

Philip was astonished. The question was impertinent in the extreme. He had a regard for Miss Abbott,
and regretted that she had been guilty of it.

"About the baby?" asked Mrs. Herriton pleasantly.

"Yes."

"As far as I know, no steps. Mrs. Theobald may
have decided on something, but I have not heard of
it."

"I was meaning, had you decided on anything?"

"The child is no relation of ours," said Philip. "It
is therefore scarcely for us to interfere."

His mother glanced at him nervously. "Poor Lilia
was almost a daughter to me once. I know what Miss
Abbott means. But now things have altered. Any initiative would naturally come from Mrs. Theobald."

"But does not Mrs. Theobald always take any
initiative from you?" asked Miss Abbott.

Mrs. Herriton could not help colouring. "I sometimes have given her advice in the past. I should not
presume to do so now."

"Then is nothing to be done for the child at all?"

"It is extraordinarily good of you to take this unexpected interest," said Philip.

"The child came into the world through my negligence," replied Miss Abbott. "It is natural I should take an interest in it."

"My dear Caroline," said Mrs. Herriton, "you must not brood over the thing. Let bygones be bygones. The child should worry you even less than it worries us. We never even mention it. It belongs to another world."

Miss Abbott got up without replying and turned to go. Her extreme gravity made Mrs. Herriton uneasy. "Of course," she added, "if Mrs. Theobald decides on any plan that seems at all practicable—I must say I don't see any such—I shall ask if I may join her in it, for Irma's sake, and share in any possible expenses."

"Please would you let me know if she decides on anything. I should like to join as well."

"My dear, how you throw about your money! We would never allow it."

"And if she decides on nothing, please also let me know. Let me know in any case."

Mrs. Herriton made a point of kissing her.

"Is the young person mad?" burst out Philip as soon as she had departed. "Never in my life have I seen such colossal impertinence. She ought to be well smacked, and sent back to Sunday-school."

His mother said nothing.

"But don't you see—she is practically threatening us? You can't put her off with Mrs. Theobald; she knows as well as we do that she is a nonentity. If we don't do anything she's going to raise a scandal—that we neglect our relatives, &c., which is, of course, a lie. Still she'll say it. Oh, dear, sweet, sober Caroline Abbott has a screw loose! We knew it at Monteriano. I had my suspicions last year one day in the train; and here it is again. The young person is mad."

She still said nothing.

"Shall I go round at once and give it her well? I'd really enjoy it."

In a low, serious voice—such a voice as she had not used to him for months—Mrs. Herriton said, "Caroline has been extremely impertinent. Yet there may be something in what she says after all. Ought the child to grow up in that place—and with that father?"

Philip started and shuddered. He saw that his mother was not sincere. Her insincerity to others had amused him, but it was disheartening when used against himself.

"Let us admit frankly," she continued, "that after all we may have responsibilities."

"I don't understand you, mother. You are turning absolutely round. What are you up to?"

In one moment an impenetrable barrier had been erected between them. They were no longer in smiling confidence. Mrs. Herriton was off on tactics of her own—tactics which might be beyond or beneath him.

His remark offended her. "Up to? I am wondering whether I ought not to adopt the child. Is that sufficiently plain?"

"And this is the result of half-a-dozen idiocies of Miss Abbott?"

"It is. I repeat, she has been extremely impertinent. None the less she is showing me my duty. If I can rescue poor Lilia's baby from that horrible man, who will bring it up either as Papist or infidel—who will certainly bring it up to be vicious—I shall do it."

"You talk like Harriet."

"And why not?" said she, flushing at what she knew to be an insult. "Say, if you choose, that I talk like Irma. That child has seen the thing more clearly than any of us. She longs for her little brother. She shall have him. I don't care if I am impulsive."

He was sure that she was not impulsive, but did not dare to say so. Her ability frightened him. All his life he had been her puppet. She let him worship Italy, and reform Sawston—just as she had let Harriet be Low Church. She had let him talk as much as he liked. But when she wanted a thing she always got it.

And though she was frightening him, she did not inspire him with reverence. Her life, he saw, was without meaning. To what purpose was her diplomacy, her insincerity, her continued repression of vigour? Did they make any one better or happier? Did they even bring happiness to herself? Harriet with her gloomy peevish creed, Lilia with her clutches after pleasure, were after all more divine than this well-ordered, active, useless machine.

Now that his mother had wounded his vanity he could criticize her thus. But he could not rebel. To the end of his days he would probably go on doing what she wanted. He watched with a cold interest the duel between her and Miss Abbott. Mrs. Herriton's policy only appeared gradually. It was to prevent Miss Abbott interfering with the child at all costs, and if possible to prevent her at a small cost. Pride was the only solid element in her disposition. She could not bear to seem less charitable than others.

"I am planning what can be done," she would tell people, "and that kind Caroline Abbott is helping me. It is no business of either of us, but we are getting to feel that the baby must not be left entirely to that horrible man. It would be unfair to little Irma; after all, he is her half-brother. No, we have come to nothing definite."

Miss Abbott was equally civil, but not to be appeased by good intentions. The child's welfare was a sacred duty to her, not a matter of pride or even of sentiment. By it alone, she felt, could she undo a little of the evil that she had permitted to come into the world. To her imagination Monteriano had become a magic city of vice, beneath whose towers no person could grow up happy or pure. Sawston, with its semi-detached houses and snobby schools, its book teas and bazaars, was certainly petty and dull; at times she found it even contemptible. But it was not a place of sin, and at Sawston, either with the Herritons or with herself, the baby should grow up.

As soon as it was inevitable, Mrs. Herriton wrote a letter for Waters and Adamson to send to Gino—the oddest letter; Philip saw a copy of it afterwards. Its ostensible purpose was to complain of the picture post-cards. Right at the end, in a few nonchalant sentences, she offered to adopt the child, provided that Gino would undertake never to come near it, and would surrender some of Lilia's money for its education.

"What do you think of it?" she asked her son. "It

would not do to let him know that we are anxious for it."

"Certainly he will never suppose that."

"But what effect will the letter have on him?"

"When he gets it he will do a sum. If it is less expensive in the long run to part with a little money and to be clear of the baby, he will part with it. If he would lose, he will adopt the tone of the loving father."

"Dear, you're shockingly cynical." After a pause she added, "How would the sum work out?"

"I don't know, I'm sure. But if you wanted to ensure the baby being posted by return, you should have sent a little sum to *him*. Oh, I'm not cynical—at least I only go by what I know of him. But I am weary of the whole show. Weary of Italy. Weary, weary, weary. Sawston's a kind, pitiful place, isn't it? I will go walk in it and seek comfort."

He smiled as he spoke, for the sake of not appearing serious. When he had left her she began to smile also.

It was to the Abbotts' that he walked. Mr. Abbott offered him tea, and Caroline, who was keeping up her Italian in the next room, came in to pour it out. He told them that his mother had written to Signor Carella, and they both uttered fervent wishes for her success.

"Very fine of Mrs. Herriton, very fine indeed," said Mr. Abbott, who, like every one else, knew nothing of his daughter's exasperating behaviour. "I'm afraid it will mean a lot of expense. She will get nothing out of Italy without paying."

"There are sure to be incidental expenses," said

Philip cautiously. Then he turned to Miss Abbott and said, "Do you suppose we shall have difficulty with the man?"

"It depends," she replied, with equal caution.

"From what you saw of him, should you conclude that he would make an affectionate parent?"

"I don't go by what I saw of him, but by what I know of him."

"Well, what do you conclude from that?"

"That he is a thoroughly wicked man."

"Yet thoroughly wicked men have loved their children. Look at Rodrigo Borgia, for example."

"I have also seen examples of that in my district."

With this remark the admirable young woman rose, and returned to keep up her Italian. She puzzled Philip extremely. He could understand enthusiasm, but she did not seem the least enthusiastic. He could understand pure cussedness, but it did not seem to be that either. Apparently she was deriving neither amusement nor profit from the struggle. Why, then, had she undertaken it? Perhaps she was not sincere. Perhaps, on the whole, that was most likely. She must be professing one thing and aiming at another. What the other thing could be he did not stop to consider. Insincerity was becoming his stock explanation for anything unfamiliar, whether that thing was a kindly action or a high ideal.

"She fences well," he said to his mother afterwards.

"What had you to fence about?" she said suavely. Her son might know her tactics, but she refused to admit that he knew. She still pretended to him that the baby was the one thing she wanted, and had always wanted, and that Miss Abbott was her valued ally.

And when, next week, the reply came from Italy, she showed him no face of triumph. "Read the letters," she said. "We have failed."

Gino wrote in his own language, but the solicitors had sent a laborious English translation, where "Preghiatissima Signora" was rendered as "Most Praiseworthy Madam," and every delicate compliment and superlative—superlatives are delicate in Italian—would have felled an ox. For a moment Philip forgot the matter in the manner; this grotesque memorial of the land he had loved moved him almost to tears. He knew the originals of these lumbering phrases; he also had sent "sincere auguries"; he also had addressed letters—who writes at home?—from the Caffè Garibaldi. "I didn't know I was still such an ass," he thought. "Why can't I realize that it's merely tricks of expression? A bounder's a bounder, whether he lives in Sawston or Monteriano."

"Isn't it disheartening?" said his mother.

He then read that Gino could not accept the generous offer. His paternal heart would not permit him to abandon this symbol of his deplored spouse. As for the picture post-cards, it displeased him greatly that they had been obnoxious. He would send no more. Would Mrs. Herriton, with her notorious kindness, explain this to Irma, and thank her for those which Irma (courteous Miss!) had sent to him?

"The sum works out against us," said Philip. "Or perhaps he is putting up the price."

"No," said Mrs. Herriton decidedly. "It is not that. For some perverse reason he will not part with

the child. I must go and tell poor Caroline. She will
be equally distressed."

She returned from the visit in the most extraordinary condition. Her face was red, she panted for
breath, there were dark circles round her eyes.

"The impudence!" she shouted. "The cursed impudence! Oh, I'm swearing. I don't care. That beastly
woman—how dare she interfere—I'll— Philip, dear,
I'm sorry. It's no good. You must go."

"Go where? Do sit down. What's happened?"
This outburst of violence from his elegant ladylike
mother pained him dreadfully. He had not known
that it was in her.

"She won't accept—won't accept the letter as final. You must go to Monteriano!"

"I won't!" he shouted back. "I've been and I've
failed. I'll never see the place again. I hate Italy."

"If you don't go, she will."

"Abbott?"

"Yes. Going alone; would start this evening. I offered to write; she said it was 'too late!' Too late! The
child, if you please—Irma's brother—to live with her,
to be brought up by her and her father at our very
gates, to go to school like a gentleman, she paying.
Oh, you're a man! It doesn't matter for you. You can
laugh. But I know what people say; and that woman
goes to Italy this evening."

He seemed to be inspired. "Then let her go! Let
her mess with Italy by herself. She'll come to grief
somehow. Italy's too dangerous, too—"

"Stop that nonsense, Philip. I will not be dis-
graced by her. I *will* have the child. Pay all we've got
for it. I will have it."

"Let her go to Italy!" he cried. "Let her meddle with what she doesn't understand! Look at this letter! The man who wrote it will marry her, or murder her, or do for her somehow. He's a bounder, but he's not an English bounder. He's mysterious and terrible. He's got a country behind him that's upset people from the beginning of the world."

"Harriet!" exclaimed his mother. "Harriet shall go too. Harriet, now, will be invaluable!" And before Philip had stopped talking nonsense, she had planned the whole thing and was looking out the trains.

Chapter Six

ITALY, PHILIP HAD always maintained, is only her true self in the height of the summer, when the tourists have left her, and her soul awakes under the beams of a vertical sun. He now had every opportunity of seeing her at her best, for it was nearly the middle of August before he went out to meet Harriet in the Tirol.

He found his sister in a dense cloud five thousand feet above the sea, chilled to the bone, overfed, bored, and not at all unwilling to be fetched away.

"It upsets one's plans terribly," she remarked, as she squeezed out her sponges, "but obviously it is my duty."

"Did mother explain it all to you?" asked Philip.

"Yes, indeed! Mother has written me a really beautiful letter. She describes how it was that she gradually got to feel that we must rescue the poor baby from its terrible surroundings, how she has tried by letter, and it is no good—nothing but insincere compliments and hypocrisy came back. Then she says, 'There is nothing like personal influence; you and Philip will succeed where I have failed.' She says, too, that Caroline Abbott has been wonderful."

Philip assented.

"Caroline feels it as keenly almost as us. That is because she knows the man. Oh, he must be loathsome! Goodness me! I've forgotten to pack the ammonia! . . . It has been a terrible lesson for Caroline, but I fancy it is her turning-point. I can't help liking to think that out of all this evil good will come."

Philip saw no prospect of good, nor of beauty either. But the expedition promised to be highly comic. He was not averse to it any longer, he was simply indifferent to all in it except the humours. These would be wonderful. Harriet, worked by her mother; Mrs. Herriton, worked by Miss Abbott; Gino, worked by a cheque—what better entertainment could he desire? There was nothing to distract him this time; his sentimentality had died, so had his anxiety for the family honour. He might be a puppet's puppet, but he knew exactly the disposition of the strings.

They travelled for thirteen hours down-hill, whilst the streams broadened and the mountains shrank, and the vegetation changed, and the people ceased being ugly and drinking beer, and began instead to drink wine and to be beautiful. And the train which had picked them at sunrise out of a waste of glaciers and hotels was waltzing at sunset round the walls of Verona.

"Absurd nonsense they talk about the heat," said

Philip, as they drove from the station. "Supposing we were here for pleasure, what could be more pleasurable than this?"

"Did you hear, though, they are remarking on the cold?" said Harriet nervously. "I should never have thought it cold."

And on the second day the heat struck them, like a hand laid over the mouth, just as they were walking to see the tomb of Juliet. From that moment everything went wrong. They fled from Verona. Harriet's sketch-book was stolen, and the bottle of ammonia in her trunk burst over her prayer-book, so that purple patches appeared on all her clothes. Then, as she was going through Mantua at four in the morning, Philip made her look out of the window because it was Virgil's birthplace, and a smut flew in her eye, and Harriet with a smut in her eye was notorious. At Bologna they stopped twenty-four hours to rest. It was a *festa*, and children blew bladder whistles night and day. "What a religion!" said Harriet. The hotel smelt, two puppies were asleep on her bed, and her bedroom window looked into a belfry, which saluted her slumbering form every quarter of an hour. Philip left his walking-stick, his socks, and the Baedeker at Bologna; she only left her sponge-bag. Next day they crossed the Apennines with a train-sick child and a hot lady, who told them that never, never before had she sweated so profusely. "Foreigners are a filthy nation," said Harriet. "I don't care if there are tunnels; open the windows." He obeyed, and she got another smut in her eye. Nor did Florence improve matters. Eating, walking, even a cross word would bathe them both in boiling water.

Philip, who was slighter of build, and less conscientious, suffered less. But Harriet had never been to Florence, and between the hours of eight and eleven she crawled like a wounded creature through the streets, and swooned before various masterpieces of art. It was an irritable couple who took tickets to Monteriano.

"Singles or returns?" said he.

"A single for me," said Harriet peevishly; "I shall never get back alive."

"Sweet creature!" said her brother, suddenly breaking down. "How helpful you will be when we come to Signor Carella!"

"Do you suppose," said Harriet, standing still among a whirl of porters—"do you suppose I am going to enter that man's house?"

"Then what have you come for, pray? For ornament?"

"To see that you do your duty."

"Oh, thanks!"

"So mother told me. For goodness sake get the tickets; here comes that hot woman again! She has the impudence to bow."

"Mother told you, did she?" said Philip wrathfully, as he went to struggle for tickets at a slit so narrow that they were handed to him edgeways. Italy was beastly, and Florence station is the centre of beastly Italy. But he had a strange feeling that he was to blame for it all; that a little influx into him of virtue would make the whole land not beastly but amusing. For there was enchantment, he was sure of that; solid enchantment, which lay behind the porters and the screaming and the dust. He could see

it in the terrific blue sky beneath which they travelled, in the whitened plain which gripped life tighter
than a frost, in the exhausted reaches of the Arno, in
the ruins of brown castles which stood quivering
upon the hills. He could see it, though his head
ached and his skin was twitching, though he was
here as a puppet, and though his sister knew how he
was here. There was nothing pleasant in that journey
to Monteriano station. But nothing—not even the
discomfort—was commonplace.

"But do people live inside?" asked Harriet. They
had exchanged railway-carriage for the legno, and the
legno had emerged from the withered trees, and had
revealed to them their destination. Philip, to be annoying, answered "No."

"What do they do there?" continued Harriet,
with a frown.

"There is a *caffè*. A prison. A theatre. A church.
Walls. A view."

"Not for me, thank you," said Harriet, after a
weighty pause.

"Nobody asked you, Miss, you see. Now Lilia
was asked by such a nice young gentleman, with
curls all over his forehead, and teeth just as white as
father makes them." Then his manner changed. "But,
Harriet, do you see nothing wonderful or attractive
in that place—nothing at all?"

"Nothing at all. It's frightful."

"I know it is. But it's old—awfully old."

"Beauty is the only test," said Harriet. "At least so
you told me when I sketched old buildings—for the
sake, I suppose, of making yourself unpleasant."

"Oh, I'm perfectly right. But at the same time—I

don't know—so many things have happened here—people have lived so hard and so splendidly—I can't explain."

"I shouldn't think you could. It doesn't seem the best moment to begin your Italy mania. I thought you were cured of it by now. Instead, will you kindly tell me what you are going to do when you arrive? I do beg you will not be taken unawares this time."

"First, Harriet, I shall settle you at the Stella d'Italia, in the comfort that befits your sex and disposition. Then I shall make myself some tea. After tea I shall take a book into Santa Deodata's, and read there. It is always fresh and cool."

The martyred Harriet exclaimed, "I'm not clever, Philip. I don't go in for it, as you know. But I know what's rude. And I know what's wrong."

"Meaning———?"

"You!" she shouted, bouncing on the cushions of the legno and startling all the fleas. "What's the good of cleverness if a man's murdered a woman?"

"Harriet, I am hot. To whom do you refer?"

"He. Her. If you don't look out he'll murder you. I wish he would."

"Tut tut, tutlet! You'd find a corpse extraordinarily inconvenient." Then he tried to be less aggravating. "I heartily dislike the fellow, but we know he didn't murder her. In that letter, though she said a lot, she never said he was physically cruel."

"He has murdered her. The things he did—things one can't even mention———"

"Things which one must mention if one's to talk at all. And things which one must keep in their proper place. Because he was unfaithful to his wife, it

doesn't follow that in every way he's absolutely vile."
He looked at the city. It seemed to approve his remark.

"It's the supreme test. The man who is unchival-
rous to a woman———"

"Oh, stow it! Take it to the Back Kitchen. It's no
more a supreme test than anything else. The Italians
never were chivalrous from the first. If you condemn
him for that, you'll condemn the whole lot."

"I condemn the whole lot."

"And the French as well?"

"And the French as well."

"Things aren't so jolly easy," said Philip, more to
himself than to her.

But for Harriet things were easy, though not jolly,
and she turned upon her brother yet again. "What
about the baby, pray? You've said a lot of smart
things and whittled away morality and religion and I
don't know what; but what about the baby? You
think me a fool, but I've been noticing you all today,
and you haven't mentioned the baby once. You
haven't thought about it, even. You don't care. Philip!
I shall not speak to you. You are intolerable."

She kept her promise, and never opened her lips
all the rest of the way. But her eyes glowed with anger and resolution. For she was a straight, brave
woman, as well as a peevish one.

Philip acknowledged her reproof to be true. He
did not care about the baby one straw. Nevertheless,
he meant to do his duty, and he was fairly confident
of success. If Gino would have sold his wife for a
thousand lire, for how much less would he not sell
his child? It was just a commercial transaction. Why

should it interfere with other things? His eyes were fixed on the towers again, just as they had been fixed when he drove with Miss Abbott. But this time his thoughts were pleasanter, for he had no such grave business on his mind. It was in the spirit of the cultivated tourist that he approached his destination.

One of the towers, rough as any other, was topped by a cross—the tower of the Collegiate Church of Santa Deodata. She was a holy maiden of the Dark Ages, the city's patron saint, and sweetness and barbarity mingle strangely in her story. So holy was she that all her life she lay upon her back in the house of her mother, refusing to eat, refusing to play, refusing to work. The devil, envious of such sanctity, tempted her in various ways. He dangled grapes above her, he showed her fascinating toys, he pushed soft pillows beneath her aching head. When all proved vain he tripped up the mother and flung her downstairs before her very eyes. But so holy was the saint that she never picked her mother up, but lay upon her back through all, and thus assured her throne in Paradise. She was only fifteen when she died, which shows how much is within the reach of any school-girl. Those who think her life was unpractical need only think of the victories upon Poggibonsi, San Gemignano, Volterra, Siena itself— all gained through the invocation of her name; they need only look at the church which rose over her grave. The grand schemes for a marble façade were never carried out, and it is brown unfinished stone until this day. But for the inside Giotto was summoned to decorate the walls of the nave. Giotto came—that is to say, he did not come, German research having decisively proved—but at all events the nave is covered with frescoes, and so are two chapels in the left transept, and the arch into the choir, and there are scraps in the choir itself. There the decoration stopped, till in the full spring of the Renaissance a great painter came to pay a few weeks' visit to his friend the Lord of Monteriano. In the intervals between the banquets and the discussions on Latin etymology and the dancing, he would stroll over to the church, and there in the fifth chapel to the right he has painted two frescoes of the death and burial of Santa Deodata. That is why Baedeker gives the place a star.

Santa Deodata was better company than Harriet, and she kept Philip in a pleasant dream until the legno drew up at the hotel. Every one there was asleep, for it was still the hour when only idiots were moving. There were not even any beggars about. The cabman put their bags down in the passage—they had left heavy luggage at the station—and strolled about till he came on the landlady's room and woke her, and sent her to them.

Then Harriet pronounced the monosyllable "Go!"

"Go where?" asked Philip, bowing to the landlady, who was swimming down the stairs.

"To the Italian. Go."

"Buona sera, signora padrona. Si ritorna volontieri a Monteriano!" (Don't be a goose. I'm not going now. You're in the way, too.) "Vorrei due camere——"

"Go. This instant. Now. I'll stand it no longer. Go!"

"I'm damned if I'll go. I want my tea."

"Swear if you like!" she cried. "Blaspheme! Abuse me! But understand, I'm in earnest."

"Harriet, don't act. Or act better."

"We've come here to get the baby back, and for nothing else. I'll not have this levity and slackness, and talk about pictures and churches. Think of mother; did she send you out for *them*?"

"Think of mother and don't straddle across the stairs. Let the cabman and the landlady come down, and let me go up and choose rooms."

"I shan't."

"Harriet, are you mad?"

"If you like. But you will not come up till you have seen the Italian."

"La signorina si sente male," said Philip, "C' è il sole."

"Poveretta!" cried the landlady and the cabman.

"Leave me alone!" said Harriet, snarling round at them. "I don't care for the lot of you. I'm English, and neither you'll come down nor he up till he goes for the baby."

"La prego—piano—piano—c è un' altra signorina che dorme——"

"We shall probably be arrested for brawling, Harriet. Have you the very slightest sense of the ludicrous?"

Harriet had not; that was why she could be so powerful. She had concocted this scene in the carriage, and nothing should baulk her of it. To the abuse in front and the coaxing behind she was equally indifferent. How long she would have stood like a glorified Horatius, keeping the staircase at both ends, was never to be known. For the young lady, whose sleep they were disturbing, awoke and opened her bedroom door, and came out on to the landing. She was Miss Abbott.

Philip's first coherent feeling was one of indignation. To be run by his mother and hectored by his sister was as much as he could stand. The intervention of a third female drove him suddenly beyond politeness. He was about to say exactly what he thought about the thing from beginning to end. But before he could do so Harriet also had seen Miss Abbott. She uttered a shrill cry of joy.

"You, Caroline, here of all people!" And in spite of the heat she darted up the stairs and imprinted an affectionate kiss upon her friend.

Philip had an inspiration. "You will have a lot to tell Miss Abbott, Harriet, and she may have as much to tell you. So I'll pay my call on Signor Carella, as you suggested, and see how things stand."

Miss Abbott uttered some noise of greeting or alarm. He did not reply to it or approach nearer to her. Without even paying the cabman, he escaped into the street.

"Tear each other's eyes out!" he cried, gesticulating at the façade of the hotel. "Give it to her, Harriet! Teach her to leave us alone. Give it to her, Caroline! Teach her to be grateful to you. Go it, ladies; go it!"

Such people as observed him were interested, but did not conclude that he was mad. This aftermath of conversation is not unknown in Italy.

He tried to think how amusing it was; but it would not do—Miss Abbott's presence affected him too personally. Either she suspected him of dishonesty, or else she was being dishonest herself. He preferred to suppose the latter. Perhaps she had seen Gino, and they had prepared some elaborate mortification for the Herritons. Perhaps Gino had sold the baby cheap to her for a joke: it was just the kind of joke that would appeal to him. Philip still remembered the laughter that had greeted his fruitless journey, and the uncouth push that had toppled him on to the bed. And whatever it might mean, Miss Abbott's presence spoilt the comedy: she would do nothing funny.

During this short meditation he had walked through the city, and was out on the other side. "Where does Signor Carella live?" he asked the men at the Dogana.

"I'll show you," said a little girl, springing out of the ground as Italian children will.

"She will show you," said the Dogana men, nodding reassuringly. "Follow her always, always, and you will come to no harm. She is a trustworthy guide.

She is my { daughter."
{ cousin."
{ sister."

Philip knew these relatives well: they ramify, if need be, all over the peninsula.

"Do you chance to know whether Signor Carella is in?" he asked her.

She had just seen him go in. Philip nodded. He was looking forward to the interview this time: it would be an intellectual duel with a man of no great intellect. What was Miss Abbott up to? That was one of the things he was going to discover. While she had it out with Harriet, he would have it out with Gino. He followed the Dogana's relative softly, like a diplomatist.

He did not follow her long, for this was the Volterra gate, and the house was exactly opposite to it. In half a minute they had scrambled down the mule-track and reached the only practicable entrance. Philip laughed, partly at the thought of Lilia in such a building, partly in the confidence of victory. Meanwhile the Dogana's relative lifted up her voice and gave a shout.

For an impressive interval there was no reply. Then the figure of a woman appeared high up on the loggia.

"That is Perfetta," said the girl.

"I want to see Signor Carella," cried Philip.

"Out!"

"Out," echoed the girl complacently.

"Why on earth did you say he was in?" He could have strangled her for temper. He had been just ripe for an interview—just the right combination of indignation and acuteness: blood hot, brain cool. But nothing ever did go right in Monteriano. "When will he be back?" he called to Perfetta. It really was too bad.

She did not know. He was away on business. He might be back this evening, he might not. He had gone to Poggibonsi.

At the sound of this word the little girl put her fingers to her nose and swept them at the plain. She sang as she did so, even as her foremothers had sung seven hundred years back—

Poggibonizzi, fatti in là,
Che Monteriano si fa città!

Then she asked Philip for a halfpenny. A German lady, friendly to the Past, had given her one that very spring.

"I shall have to leave a message," he called.

"Now Perfetta has gone for her basket," said the little girl. "When she returns she will lower it—so. Then you will put your card into it. Then she will raise it—thus. By this means——"

When Perfetta returned, Philip remembered to ask after the baby. It took longer to find than the basket, and he stood perspiring in the evening sun, trying to avoid the smell of the drains and to prevent the little girl from singing against Poggibonsi. The olive-trees beside him were draped with the weekly—or more probably the monthly—wash. What a frightful spotty blouse! He could not think where he had seen it. Then he remembered that it was Lilia's. She had brought it "to hack about in" at Sawston, and had taken it to Italy because "in Italy anything does." He had rebuked her for the sentiment.

"Beautiful as an angel!" bellowed Perfetta, holding out something which must be Lilia's baby. "But who am I addressing?"

"Thank you—here is my card." He had written on it a civil request to Gino for an interview next morning. But before he placed it in the basket and revealed his identity, he wished to find something out. "Has a young lady happened to call here lately—a young English lady?"

Perfetta begged his pardon: she was a little deaf.

"A young lady—pale, large, tall."

She did not quite catch.

"A YOUNG LADY!"

"Perfetta is deaf when she chooses," said the Dogana's relative. At last Philip admitted the peculiarity and strode away. He paid off the detestable child at the Volterra gate. She got two nickel pieces and was not pleased, partly because it was too much, partly because he did not look pleased when he gave it to her. He caught her fathers and cousins winking at each other as he walked past them. Monteriano seemed in one conspiracy to make him look a fool. He felt tired and anxious and muddled, and not sure of anything except that his temper was lost. In this mood he returned to the Stella d'Italia, and there, as he was ascending the stairs, Miss Abbott popped out of the dining-room on the first floor and beckoned to him mysteriously.

"I was going to make myself some tea," he said, with his hand still on the banisters.

"I should be grateful——"

So he followed her into the dining-room and shut the door.

"You see," she began, "Harriet knows nothing."

"No more do I. He was out."

"But what's that to do with it?"

He presented her with an unpleasant smile. She fenced well, as he had noticed before. "He was out. You find me as ignorant as you have left Harriet."

"What do you mean? Please, please Mr. Herriton, don't be mysterious: there isn't the time. Any moment Harriet may be down, and we shan't have decided how to behave to her. Sawston was different: we had to keep up appearances. But here we must speak out, and I think I can trust you to do it. Otherwise we'll never start clear."

"Pray let us start clear," said Philip, pacing up and down the room. "Permit me to begin by asking you a question. In which capacity have you come to Monteriano—spy or traitor?"

"Spy!" she answered, without a moment's hesitation. She was standing by the little Gothic window as she spoke—the hotel had been a palace once—and with her finger she was following the curves of the moulding as if they might feel beautiful and strange. "Spy," she repeated, for Philip was bewildered at learning her guilt so easily, and could not answer a word. "Your mother has behaved dishonourably all through. She never wanted the child; no harm in that; but she is too proud to let it come to me. She has done all she could to wreck things; she did not tell you everything; she has told Harriet nothing at all; she has lied or acted lies everywhere. I cannot trust your mother. So I have come here alone—all across Europe; no one knows it; my father thinks I am in Normandy—to spy on Mrs. Herriton. Don't let's argue!" for he had begun, almost mechanically, to rebuke her for impertinence. "If you are here to get the child, I will help you; if you are here to fail, I shall get it instead of you."

"It is hopeless to expect you to believe me," he stammered. "But I can assert that we are here to get the child, even if it costs us all we've got. My mother has fixed no money limit whatever. I am here to carry out her instructions. I think that you will ap-

prove of them, as you have practically dictated them.
I do not approve of them. They are absurd."

She nodded carelessly. She did not mind what he
said. All she wanted was to get the baby out of
Monteriano.

"Harriet also carries out your instructions," he
continued. "She, however, approves of them, and
does not know that they proceed from you. I think,
Miss Abbott, you had better take entire charge of the
rescue party. I have asked for an interview with Signor Carella tomorrow morning. Do you acquiesce?"

She nodded again.

"Might I ask for details of your interview with
him? They might be helpful to me."

He had spoken at random. To his delight she
suddenly collapsed. Her hand fell from the window.
Her face was red with more than the reflection of
evening.

"My interview—how do you know of it?"

"From Perfetta, if it interests you."

"Who ever is Perfetta?"

"The woman who must have let you in."

"In where?"

"Into Signor Carella's house."

"Mr. Herriton!" she exclaimed. "How could you
believe her? Do you suppose that I would have entered that man's house, knowing about him all that I
do? I think you have very odd ideas of what is possible for a lady. I hear you wanted Harriet to go. Very
properly she refused. Eighteen months ago I might
have done such a thing. But I trust I have learnt how
to behave by now."

Philip began to see that there were two Miss

Abbotts—the Miss Abbott who could travel alone to Monteriano, and the Miss Abbott who could not enter Gino's house when she got there. It was an amusing discovery. Which of them would respond to his next move?

"I suppose I misunderstood Perfetta. Where did you have your interview, then?"

"Not an interview—an accident—I am very sorry—I meant you to have the chance of seeing him first. Though it is your fault. You are a day late. You were due here yesterday. So I came yesterday, and, not finding you, went up to the Rocca—you know that kitchen-garden where they let you in, and there is a ladder up to a broken tower, where you can stand and see all the other towers below you and the plain and all the other hills?"

"Yes, yes. I know the Rocca; I told you of it."

"So I went up in the evening for the sunset: I had nothing to do. He was in the garden: it belongs to a friend of his."

"And you talked."

"It was very awkward for me. But I had to talk: he seemed to make me. You see he thought I was here as a tourist; he thinks so still. He intended to be civil, and I judged it better to be civil also."

"And of what did you talk?"

"The weather—there will be rain, he says, by tomorrow evening—the other towns, England, myself, about you a little, and he actually mentioned Lilia. He was perfectly disgusting; he pretended he loved her; he offered to show me her grave—the grave of the woman he has murdered!"

"My dear Miss Abbott, he is not a murderer. I

have just been driving that into Harriet. And when you know the Italians as well as I do, you will realize that in all that he said to you he was perfectly sincere. The Italians are essentially dramatic; they look on death and love as spectacles. I don't doubt that he persuaded himself, for the moment, that he had behaved admirably, both as husband and widower."

"You may be right," said Miss Abbott, impressed for the first time. "When I tried to pave the way, so to speak—to hint that he had not behaved as he ought—well, it was no good at all. He couldn't or wouldn't understand."

There was something very humorous in the idea of Miss Abbott approaching Gino, on the Rocca, in the spirit of a district visitor. Philip, whose temper was returning, laughed.

"Harriet would say he has no sense of sin."

"Harriet may be right, I am afraid."

"If so, perhaps he isn't sinful!"

Miss Abbott was not one to encourage levity. "I know what he has done," she said. "What he says and what he thinks is of very little importance."

Philip smiled at her crudity. "I should like to hear, though, what he said about me. Is he preparing a warm reception?"

"Oh, no, not that. I never told him that you and Harriet were coming. You could have taken him by surprise if you liked. He only asked for you, and wished he hadn't been so rude to you eighteen months ago."

"What a memory the fellow has for little things!" He turned away as he spoke, for he did not want her to see his face. It was suffused with pleasure. For an apology, which would have been intolerable eighteen months ago, was gracious and agreeable now.

She would not let this pass. "You did not think it a little thing at the time. You told me he had assaulted you."

"I lost my temper," said Philip lightly. His vanity had been appeased, and he knew it. This tiny piece of civility had changed his mood. "Did he really—what exactly did he say?"

"He said he was sorry—pleasantly, as Italians do say such things. But he never mentioned the baby once."

What did the baby matter when the world was suddenly right way up? Philip smiled, and was shocked at himself for smiling, and smiled again. For romance had come back to Italy; there were no cads in her; she was beautiful, courteous, lovable, as of old. And Miss Abbott—she, too, was beautiful in her way, for all her gaucheness and conventionality. She really cared about life, and tried to live it properly. And Harriet—even Harriet tried.

This admirable change in Philip proceeds from nothing admirable, and may therefore provoke the gibes of the cynical. But angels and other practical people will accept it reverently, and write it down as good.

"The view from the Rocca (small gratuity) is finest at sunset," he murmured, more to himself than to her.

"And he never mentioned the baby once," Miss Abbott repeated. But she had returned to the window, and again her finger pursued the delicate curves. He watched her in silence, and was more attracted to her than he had ever been before. She really was the strangest mixture.

"The view from the Rocca—wasn't it fine?"

"What isn't fine here?" she answered gently, and then added, "I wish I was Harriet," throwing an extraordinary meaning into the words.

"Because Harriet——?"

She would not go further, but he believed that she had paid homage to the complexity of life. For her, at all events, the expedition was neither easy nor jolly. Beauty, evil, charm, vulgarity, mystery—she also acknowledged this tangle, in spite of herself. And her voice thrilled him when she broke silence with "Mr. Herriton—come here—look at this!"

She removed a pile of plates from the Gothic window, and they leant out of it. Close opposite, wedged between mean houses, there rose up one of the great towers. It is your tower: you stretch a barricade between it and the hotel, and the traffic is blocked in a moment. Farther up, where the street empties out by the church, your connections, the Merli and the Capocchi, do likewise. They command the Piazza, you the Siena gate. No one can move in either but he shall be instantly slain, either by bows or by crossbows, or by Greek fire. Beware, however, of the back bedroom windows. For they are menaced by the tower of the Aldobrandeschi, and before now arrows have stuck quivering over the washstand. Guard these windows well, lest there be a repetition of the events of February 1338, when the hotel was surprised from the rear, and your dearest friend—you could just make out that it was he—was thrown at you over the stairs.

"It reaches up to heaven," said Philip, "and down to the other place." The summit of the tower was radiant in the sun, while its base was in shadow and pasted over with advertisements. "Is it to be a symbol of the town?"

She gave no hint that she understood him. But they remained together at the window because it was a little cooler and so pleasant. Philip found a certain grace and lightness in his companion which he had never noticed in England. She was appallingly narrow, but her consciousness of wider things gave to her narrowness a pathetic charm. He did not suspect that he was more graceful too. For our vanity is such that we hold our own characters immutable, and we are slow to acknowledge that they have changed, even for the better.

Citizens came out for a little stroll before dinner. Some of them stood and gazed at the advertisements on the tower.

"Surely that isn't an opera-bill?" said Miss Abbott.

Philip put on his pince-nez. " 'Lucia di Lammermoor. By the Master Donizetti. Unique representation. This evening.' "

"But is there an opera? Right up here?"

"Why, yes. These people know how to live. They would sooner have a thing bad than not have it at all. That is why they have got to have so much that is good. However bad the performance is tonight, it will be alive. Italians don't love music silently, like the beastly Germans. The audience takes its share— sometimes more."

"Can't we go?"

He turned on her, but not unkindly. "But we're here to rescue a child!"

He cursed himself for the remark. All the pleasure and the light went out of her face, and she became again Miss Abbott of Sawston—good, oh, most undoubtedly good, but most appallingly dull. Dull and remorseful: it is a deadly combination, and he strove against it in vain till he was interrupted by the opening of the dining-room door.

They started as guiltily as if they had been flirting. Their interview had taken such an unexpected course. Anger, cynicism, stubborn morality—all had ended in a feeling of good-will towards each other and towards the city which had received them. And now Harriet was here—acrid, indissoluble, large; the same in Italy as in England—changing her disposition never, and her atmosphere under protest.

Yet even Harriet was human, and the better for a little tea. She did not scold Philip for finding Gino out, as she might reasonably have done. She showered civilities on Miss Abbott, exclaiming again and again that Caroline's visit was one of the most fortunate coincidences in the world. Caroline did not contradict her.

"You see him tomorrow at ten, Philip. Well, don't forget the blank cheque. Say an hour for the business. No, Italians are so slow; say two. Twelve o'clock. Lunch. Well—then it's no good going till the evening train. I can manage the baby as far as Florence——"

"My dear sister, you can't run on like that. You don't buy a pair of gloves in two hours, much less a baby."

"Three hours, then, or four; or make him learn English ways. At Florence we get a nurse——"

"But, Harriet," said Miss Abbott, "what if at first he was to refuse?"

"I don't know the meaning of the word," said Harriet impressively. "I've told the landlady that Philip and I only want our rooms one night, and we shall keep to it."

"I dare say it will be all right. But, as I told you, I thought the man I met on the Rocca a strange, difficult man."

"He's insolent to ladies, we know. But my brother can be trusted to bring him to his senses. That woman, Philip, whom you saw will carry the baby to the hotel. Of course you must tip her for it. And try, if you can, to get poor Lilia's silver bangles. They were nice quiet things, and will do for Irma. And there is an inlaid box I lent her—lent, not gave—to keep her handkerchiefs in. It's of no real value; but this is our only chance. Don't ask for it; but if you see it lying about, just say——"

"No, Harriet; I'll try for the baby, but for nothing else. I promise to do that tomorrow, and to do it in the way you wish. But tonight, as we're all tired, we want a change of topic. We want relaxation. We want to go to the theatre."

"Theatres here? And at such a moment?"

"We should hardly enjoy it, with the great interview impending," said Miss Abbott, with an anxious glance at Philip.

He did not betray her, but said, "Don't you think it's better than sitting in all the evening and getting nervous?"

His sister shook her head. "Mother wouldn't like it. It would be most unsuitable—almost irreverent. Besides all that, foreign theatres are notorious. Don't you remember those letters in the 'Church Family Newspaper'?"

"But this is an opera—'Lucia di Lammermoor'—Sir Walter Scott—classical, you know."

Harriet's face grew resigned. "Certainly one has so few opportunities of hearing music. It is sure to be very bad. But it might be better than sitting idle all the evening. We have no book, and I lost my crochet at Florence."

"Good. Miss Abbott, you are coming too?"

"It is very kind of you, Mr. Herriton. In some ways I should enjoy it; but—excuse the suggestion—I don't think we ought to go to cheap seats."

"Good gracious me!" cried Harriet, "I should never have thought of that. As likely as not, we should have tried to save money and sat among the most awful people. One keeps on forgetting this is Italy."

"Unfortunately I have no evening dress; and if the seats——"

"Oh, that'll be all right," said Philip, smiling at his timorous, scrupulous women-kind. "We'll go as we are, and buy the best we can get. Monteriano is not formal."

So this strenuous day of resolutions, plans, alarms, battles, victories, defeats, truces, ended at the opera. Miss Abbott and Harriet were both a little shame-faced. They thought of their friends at Sawston, who were supposing them to be now tilting against the powers of evil. What would Mrs.

Herriton, or Irma, or the curates at the Back Kitchen say if they could see the rescue party at a place of amusement on the very first day of its mission? Philip, too, marvelled at his wish to go. He began to see that he was enjoying his time in Monteriano, in spite of the tiresomeness of his companions and the occasional contrariness of himself.

He had been to this theatre many years before, on the occasion of a performance of "La Zia di Carlo." Since then it had been thoroughly done up, in the tints of the beet-root and the tomato, and was in many other ways a credit to the little town. The orchestra had been enlarged, some of the boxes had terra-cotta draperies, and over each box was now suspended an enormous tablet, neatly framed, bearing upon it the number of that box. There was also a drop-scene, representing a pink and purple landscape, wherein sported many a lady lightly clad, and two more ladies lay along the top of the proscenium to steady a large and pallid clock. So rich and so appalling was the effect, that Philip could scarcely suppress a cry. There is something majestic in the bad taste of Italy; it is not the bad taste of a country which knows no better; it has not the nervous vulgarity of England, or the blinded vulgarity of Germany. It observes beauty, and chooses to pass it by. But it attains to beauty's confidence. This tiny theatre of Monteriano spraddled and swaggered with the best of them, and these ladies with their clock would have nodded to the young men on the ceiling of the Sistine.

Philip had tried for a box, but all the best were taken: it was rather a grand performance, and he had to be content with stalls. Harriet was fretful and insular. Miss Abbott was pleasant, and insisted on praising everything: her only regret was that she had no pretty clothes with her.

"We do all right," said Philip, amused at her unwonted vanity.

"Yes, I know; but pretty things pack as easily as ugly ones. We had no need to come to Italy like guys."

This time he did not reply. "But we're here to rescue a baby." For he saw a charming picture, as charming a picture as he had seen for years—the hot red theatre; outside the theatre, towers and dark gates and mediaeval walls; beyond the walls olive-trees in the starlight and white winding roads and fireflies and untroubled dust; and here in the middle of it all, Miss Abbott, wishing she had not come looking like a guy. She had made the right remark. Most undoubtedly she had made the right remark. This stiff suburban woman was unbending before the shrine.

"Don't you like it at all?" he asked her.

"Most awfully." And by this bald interchange they convinced each other that Romance was here.

Harriet, meanwhile, had been coughing ominously at the drop-scene, which presently rose on the grounds of Ravenswood, and the chorus of Scotch retainers burst into cry. The audience accompanied with tapping and drummings, swaying in the melody like corn in the wind. Harriet, though she did not care for music, knew how to listen to it. She uttered an acid "Shish!"

"Shut it," whispered her brother.

"We must make a stand from the beginning. They're talking."

"It is tiresome," murmured Miss Abbott; "but perhaps it isn't for us to interfere."

Harriet shook her head and shished again. The people were quiet, not because it is wrong to talk during a chorus, but because it is natural to be civil to a visitor. For a little time she kept the whole house in order, and could smile at her brother complacently.

Her success annoyed him. He had grasped the principle of opera in Italy—it aims not at illusion but at entertainment—and he did not want this great evening-party to turn into a prayer-meeting. But soon the boxes began to fill, and Harriet's power was over. Families greeted each other across the auditorium. People in the pit hailed their brothers and sons in the chorus, and told them how well they were singing. When Lucia appeared by the fountain there was loud applause, and cries of "Welcome to Monteriano!"

"Ridiculous babies!" said Harriet, settling down in her stall.

"Why, it is the famous hot lady of the Apennines," cried Philip; "the one who had never, never before——"

"Ugh! Don't. She will be very vulgar. And I'm sure it's even worse here than in the tunnel. I wish we'd never——"

Lucia began to sing, and there was a moment's silence. She was stout and ugly; but her voice was still beautiful, and as she sang the theatre murmured like a hive of happy bees. All through the *coloratura* she was accompanied by sighs, and its top note was drowned in a shout of universal joy.

So the opera proceeded. The singers drew inspiration from the audience, and the two great sextettes were rendered not unworthily. Miss Abbott fell into the spirit of the thing. She, too, chatted and laughed and applauded and encored, and rejoiced in the existence of beauty. As for Philip, he forgot himself as well as his mission. He was not even an enthusiastic visitor. For he had been in this place always. It was his home.

Harriet, like M. Bovary on a more famous occasion, was trying to follow the plot. Occasionally she nudged her companions, and asked them what had become of Walter Scott. She looked round grimly. The audience sounded drunk, and even Caroline, who never took a drop, was swaying oddly. Violent waves of excitement, all arising from very little, went sweeping round the theatre. The climax was reached in the mad scene. Lucia, clad in white, as befitted her malady, suddenly gathered up her streaming hair and bowed her acknowledgment to the audience. Then from the back of the stage—she feigned not to see it—there advanced a kind of bamboo clothes-horse, struck all over with bouquets. It was very ugly, and most of the flowers in it were false. Lucia knew this, and so did the audience; and they all knew that the clothes-horse was a piece of stage property, brought in to make the performance go year after year. None the less did it unloose the great deeps. With a scream of amazement and joy she embraced the animal, pulled out one or two practicable blossoms, pressed them to her lips, and flung them into her admirers.

They flung them back, with loud melodious cries, and a little boy in one of the stageboxes snatched up his sister's carnations and offered them. "Che carino!" exclaimed the singer. She darted at the little boy and kissed him. Now the noise became tremendous. "Silence! silence!" shouted many old gentlemen behind. "Let the divine creature continue!" But the young men in the adjacent box were imploring Lucia to extend her civility to them. She refused, with a humorous, expressive gesture. One of them hurled a bouquet at her. She spurned it with her foot. Then, encouraged by the roars of the audience, she picked it up and tossed it to them. Harriet was always unfortunate. The bouquet struck her full in the chest, and a little billet-doux fell out of it into her lap.

"Call this classical!" she cried, rising from her seat. "It's not even respectable! Philip! take me out at once."

"Whose is it?" shouted her brother, holding up the bouquet in one hand and the billet-doux in the other. "Whose is it?"

The house exploded, and one of the boxes was violently agitated, as if some one was being hauled to the front. Harriet moved down the gangway, and compelled Miss Abbott to follow her. Philip, still laughing and calling "Whose is it?" brought up the rear. He was drunk with excitement. The heat, the fatigue, and the enjoyment had mounted into his head.

"To the left!" the people cried. "The innamorato is to the left."

He deserted his ladies and plunged towards the

box. A young man was flung stomach downwards across the balustrade. Philip handed him up the bouquet and the note. Then his own hands were seized affectionately. It all seemed quite natural.

"Why have you not written?" cried the young man. "Why do you take me by surprise?"

"Oh, I've written," said Philip hilariously. "I left a note this afternoon."

"Silence! silence!" cried the audience, who were beginning to have enough. "Let the divine creature continue." Miss Abbott and Harriet had disappeared.

"No! no!" cried the young man. "You don't escape me now." For Philip was trying feebly to disengage his hands. Amiable youths bent out of the box and invited him to enter it.

"Gino's friend are ours——"

"Friends?" cried Gino. "A relative! A brother! Fra Filippo, who has come all the way from England and never written."

"I left a message."

The audience began to hiss.

"Come in to us."

"Thank you—ladies—there is not time——"

The next moment he was swinging by his arms. The moment after he shot over the balustrade into the box. Then the conductor, seeing that the incident was over, raised his baton. The house was hushed, and Lucia di Lammermoor resumed her song of madness and death.

Philip had whispered introductions to the pleasant people who had pulled him in—tradesmen's sons perhaps they were, or medical students, or solicitors' clerks, or sons of other dentists. There is no knowing who is who in Italy. The guest of the evening was a private soldier. He shared the honour now with Philip. The two had to stand side by side in the front, and exchange compliments, whilst Gino presided, courteous, but delightfully familiar. Philip would have a spasm of horror at the muddle he had made. But the spasm would pass, and again he would be enchanted by the kind, cheerful voices, the laughter that was never vapid, and the light caress of the arm across his back.

He could not get away till the play was nearly finished, and Edgardo was singing amongst the tombs of ancestors. His new friends hoped to see him at the Garibaldi tomorrow evening. He promised; then he remembered that if they kept to Harriet's plan he would have left Monteriano. "At ten o'clock, then," he said to Gino. "I want to speak to you alone. At ten."

"Certainly!" laughed the other.

Miss Abbott was sitting up for him when he got back. Harriet, it seemed, had gone straight to bed.

"That was he, wasn't it?" she asked.

"Yes, rather."

"I suppose you didn't settle anything?"

"Why, no; how could I? The fact is—well, I got taken by surprise, but after all, what does it matter? There's no earthly reason why we shouldn't do the business pleasantly. He's a perfectly charming person, and so are his friends. I'm his friend now—his long-lost brother. What's the harm? I tell you, Miss Abbott, it's one thing for England and another for Italy. There we plan and get on high moral horses. Here we find what asses we are, for things go off quite easily, all by themselves. My hat, what a night! Did you ever see a really purple sky and really silver stars before? Well, as I was saying, it's absurd to worry; he's not a porky father. He wants that baby as little as I do. He's been ragging my dear mother—just as he ragged me eighteen months ago, and I've forgiven him. Oh, but he has a sense of humour!"

Miss Abbott, too, had a wonderful evening, nor did she ever remember such stars or such a sky. Her head, too, was full of music, and that night when she opened the window her room was filled with warm, sweet air. She was bathed in beauty within and without; she could not go to bed for happiness. Had she ever been so happy before? Yes, once before, and here, a night in March, the night Gino and Lilia had told her of their love—the night whose evil she had come now to undo.

She gave a sudden cry of shame. "This time—the same place—the same thing"—and she began to beat down her happiness, knowing it to be sinful. She was here to fight against this place, to rescue a little soul who was innocent as yet. She was here to champion morality and purity, and the holy life of an English home. In the spring she had sinned through ignorance; she was not ignorant now. "Help me!" she cried, and shut the window as if there was magic in the encircling air. But the tunes would not go out of her head, and all night long she was troubled by torrents of music, and by applause and laughter, and angry young men who shouted the distich out of Baedeker:—

Poggibonizzi fatti in là,
Che Monteriano si fa città!

Poggibonsi was revealed to her as they sang—a joy-
less, straggling place, full of people who pretended.
When she woke up she knew that it had been
Sawston.

Chapter Seven

AT ABOUT NINE o'clock next morning Perfetta went out on to the loggia, not to look at the view, but to throw some dirty water at it. "Scusì tanto!" she wailed, for the water spattered a tall young lady who had for some time been tapping at the lower door.

"Is Signor Carella in?" the young lady asked. It was no business of Perfetta's to be shocked, and the style of the visitor seemed to demand the reception-room. Accordingly she opened its shutters, dusted a round patch on one of the horsehair chairs, and bade the lady do herself the inconvenience of sitting down. Then she ran into Monteriano and shouted up and down its streets until such time as her young master should hear her.

The reception-room was sacred to the dead wife. Her shiny portrait hung upon the wall—similar, doubtless, in all respects to the one which would be pasted on her tombstone. A little piece of black drapery had been tacked above the frame to lend a dignity to woe. But two of the tacks had fallen out, and the effect was now rakish, as of a drunkard's bonnet. A coon song lay open on the piano, and of the two tables one supported Baedeker's "Central Italy," the other Harriet's inlaid box. And over everything there lay a deposit of heavy white dust, which was only blown off one moment to thicken on another. It is well to be remembered with love. It is not so very dreadful to be forgotten entirely. But if we shall resent anything on earth at all, we shall resent the consecration of a deserted room.

Miss Abbott did not sit down, partly because the antimacassars might harbour fleas, partly because she had suddenly felt faint, and was glad to cling on to the funnel of the stove. She struggled with herself, for she had need to be very calm; only if she was very calm might her behaviour be justified. She had broken faith with Philip and Harriet: she was going to try for the baby before they did. If she failed she could scarcely look them in the face again.

"Harriet and her brother," she reasoned, "don't realize what is before them. She would bluster and be rude; he would be pleasant and take it as a joke. Both of them—even if they offered money—would fail. But I begin to understand the man's nature; he does not love the child, but he will be touchy about it—and that is quite as bad for us. He's charming, but he's no fool; he conquered me last year; he conquered Mr. Herriton yesterday, and if I am not careful he will conquer us all today, and the baby will grow up in Monteriano. He is terribly strong; Lilia found that out, but only I remember it now."

This attempt, and this justification of it, were the results of the long and restless night. Miss Abbott had come to believe that she alone could do battle with Gino, because she alone understood him; and she had put this, as nicely as she could, in a note which she had left for Philip. It distressed her to write such a note, partly because her education inclined her to reverence the male, partly because she had got to like Philip a good deal after their last strange interview. His pettiness would be dispersed, and as for his "unconventionality," which was so much gossiped about at Sawston, she began to see that it did not differ greatly from certain familiar notions of her own. If only he would forgive her for what she was doing now, there might perhaps be before them a long and profitable friendship. But she must succeed. No one would forgive her if she did not succeed. She prepared to do battle with the powers of evil.

The voice of her adversary was heard at last, singing fearlessly from his expanded lungs, like a professional. Herein he differed from Englishmen, who always have a little feeling against music, and sing only from the throat, apologetically. He padded upstairs, and looked in at the open door of the reception-room without seeing her. Her heart leapt and her throat was dry when he turned away and passed, still singing, into the room opposite. It is alarming not to be seen.

He had left the door of this room open, and she could see into it, right across the landing. It was in a shocking mess. Food, bedclothes, patent-leather boots, dirty plates, and knives lay strewn over a large table and on the floor. But it was the mess that comes of life, not of desolation. It was preferable to the charnel-chamber in which she was standing now, and the light in it was soft and large, as from some gracious, noble opening.

He stopped singing, and cried "Where is Perfetta?"

His back was turned, and he was lighting a cigar. He was not speaking to Miss Abbott. He could not even be expecting her. The vista of the landing and the two open doors made him both remote and significant, like an actor on the stage, intimate and unapproachable at the same time. She could no more call out to him than if he was Hamlet.

"You know!" he continued, "but you will not tell me. Exactly like you." He reclined on the table and blew a fat smoke-ring. "And why won't you tell me the numbers? I have dreamt of a red hen—that is two hundred and five, and a friend unexpected—he means eighty-two. But I try for the Terno this week. So tell me another number."

Miss Abbott did not know of the Tombola. His speech terrified her. She felt those subtle restrictions which come upon us in fatigue. Had she slept well she would have greeted him as soon as she saw him. Now it was impossible. He had got into another world.

She watched his smoke-ring. The air had carried it slowly away from him, and brought it out intact upon the landing.

"Two hundred and five—eighty-two. In any case

I shall put them on Bari, not on Florence. I cannot tell you why; I have a feeling this week for Bari." Again she tried to speak. But the ring mesmerized her. It had become vast and elliptical, and floated in at the reception-room door.

"Ah! you don't care if you get the profits. You won't even say 'Thank you, Gino.' Say it, or I'll drop hot, red-hot ashes on you. 'Thank you, Gino——' "

The ring had extended its pale blue coils towards her. She lost self-control. It enveloped her. As if it was a breath from the pit, she screamed.

There he was, wanting to know what had frightened her, how she had got here, why she had never spoken. He made her sit down. He brought her wine, which she refused. She had not one word to say to him.

"What is it?" he repeated. "What has frightened you?"

He, too, was frightened, and perspiration came starting through the tan. For it is a serious thing to have been watched. We all radiate something curiously intimate when we believe ourselves to be alone.

"Business——" she said at last.

"Business with me?"

"Most important business." She was lying, white and limp, in the dusty chair.

"Before business you must get well; this is the best wine."

She refused it feebly. He poured out a glass. She drank it. As she did so she became self-conscious. However important the business, it was not proper of her to have called on him, or to accept his hospitality.

"Perhaps you are engaged," she said. "And as I am not very well——"

"You are not well enough to go back. And I am not engaged."

She looked nervously at the other room.

"Ah, now I understand," he exclaimed. "Now I see what frightened you. But why did you never speak?" And taking her into the room where he lived, he pointed to—the baby.

She had thought so much about this baby, of its welfare, its soul, its morals, its probable defects. But, like most unmarried people, she had only thought of it as a word—just as the healthy man only thinks of the word death, not of death itself. The real thing, lying asleep on a dirty rug, disconcerted her. It did not stand for a principle any longer. It was so much flesh and blood, so many inches and ounces of life—a glorious, unquestionable fact, which a man and another woman had given to the world. You could talk to it; in time it would answer you; in time it would not answer you unless it chose, but would secrete, within the compass of its body, thoughts and wonderful passions of its own. And this was the machine on which she and Mrs. Herriton and Philip and Harriet had for the last month been exercising their various ideals—had determined that in time it should move this way or that way, should accomplish this and not that. It was to be Low Church, it was to be high-principled, it was to be tactful, gentlemanly, artistic—excellent things all. Yet now that she saw this baby, lying asleep on a dirty rug, she had a great disposition not to dictate one of them, and to exert no more influence than there may be in a kiss or in the vaguest of the heartfelt prayers.

But she had practised self-discipline, and her thoughts and actions were not yet to correspond. To recover her self-esteem she tried to imagine that she was in her district, and to behave accordingly.

"What a fine child, Signor Carella. And how nice of you to talk to it. Though I see that the ungrateful little fellow is asleep! Seven months? No, eight; of course eight. Still, he is a remarkably fine child for his age."

Italian is a bad medium for condescension. The patronizing words came out gracious and sincere, and he smiled with pleasure.

"You must not stand. Let us sit on the loggia, where it is cool. I am afraid the room is very untidy," he added, with the air of a hostess who apologizes for a stray thread on the drawing-room carpet. Miss Abbott picked her way to the chair. He sat near her, astride the parapet, with one foot in the loggia and the other dangling into the view. His face was in profile, and its beautiful contours drove artfully against the misty green of the opposing hills. "Posing!" said Miss Abbott to herself. "A born artist's model."

"Mr. Herriton called yesterday," she began, "but you were out."

He started an elaborate and graceful explanation. He had gone for the day to Poggibonsi. Why had the Herritons not written to him, so that he could have received them properly? Poggibonsi would have done any day; not but what his business there was fairly important. What did she suppose that it was?

Naturally she was not greatly interested. She had not come from Sawston to guess why he had been to Poggibonsi. She answered politely that she had no idea, and returned to her mission.

"But guess!" he persisted, clapping the balustrade between his hands.

She suggested, with gentle sarcasm, that perhaps he had gone to Poggibonsi to find something to do.

He intimated that it was not as important as all that. Something to do—an almost hopeless quest! "E manca questo!" He rubbed his thumb and forefinger together, to indicate that he had no money. Then he sighed, and blew another smoke-ring. Miss Abbott took heart and turned diplomatic.

"This house," she said, "is a large house."

"Exactly," was his gloomy reply. "And when my poor wife died——" He got up, went in, and walked across the landing to the reception-room door, which he closed reverently. Then he shut the door of the living-room with his foot, returned briskly to his seat, and continued his sentence. "When my poor wife died I thought of having my relatives to live here. My father wished to give up his practice at Empoli; my mother and sisters and two aunts were also willing. But it was impossible. They have their ways of doing things, and when I was younger I was content with them. But now I am a man. I have my own ways. Do you understand?"

"Yes, I do," said Miss Abbott, thinking of her own dear father, whose tricks and habits, after twenty-five years spent in their company, were beginning to get on her nerves. She remembered, though, that she was not here to sympathize with Gino—at all events, not to show that she sympathized. She also reminded herself that he was not worthy of sympathy. "It is a large house," she repeated.

"Immense; and the taxes! But it will be better when—— Ah! but you have never guessed why I went to Poggibonsi—why it was that I was out when he called."

"I cannot guess, Signor Carella. I am here on business."

"But try."

"I cannot; I hardly know you."

"But we are old friends," he said, "and your approval will be grateful to me. You gave it me once before. Will you give it now?"

"I have not come as a friend this time," she answered stiffly. "I am not likely, Signor Carella, to approve of anything you do."

"Oh, Signorina!" He laughed, as if he found her piquant and amusing. "Surely you approve of marriage?"

"Where there is love," said Miss Abbott, looking at him hard. His face had altered in the last year, but not for the worse, which was baffling.

"Where there is love," said he, politely echoing the English view. Then he smiled on her, expecting congratulations.

"Do I understand that you are proposing to marry again?"

He nodded.

"I forbid you, then!"

He looked puzzled, but took it for some foreign banter, and laughed.

"I forbid you!" repeated Miss Abbott, and all the indignation of her sex and her nationality went thrilling through the words.

"But why?" He jumped up, frowning. His voice was squeaky and petulant, like that of a child who is suddenly forbidden a toy.

"You have ruined one woman; I forbid you to ruin another. It is not a year since Lilia died. You pretended to me the other day that you loved her. It is a lie. You wanted her money. Has this woman money too?"

"Why, yes!" he said irritably. "A little."

"And I suppose you will say that you love her."

"I shall not say it. It will be untrue. Now my poor wife——" He stopped, seeing that the comparison would involve him in difficulties. And indeed he had often found Lilia as agreeable as any one else.

Miss Abbott was furious at this final insult to her dead acquaintance. She was glad that after all she could be so angry with the boy. She glowed and throbbed; her tongue moved nimbly. At the finish, if the real business of the day had been completed, she could have swept majestically from the house. But the baby still remained, asleep on a dirty rug.

Gino was thoughtful, and stood scratching his head. He respected Miss Abbott. He wished that she would respect him. "So you do not advise me?" he said dolefully. "But why should it be a failure?"

Miss Abbott tried to remember that he was really

a child still—a child with the strength and the passions of a disreputable man. "How can it succeed," she said solemnly, "where there is no love?"

"But she does love me! I forgot to tell you that."

"Indeed."

"Passionately." He laid his hand upon his own heart.

"Then God help her!"

He stamped impatiently. "Whatever I say displeases you, Signorina. God help you, for you are most unfair. You say that I ill-treated my dear wife. It is not so. I have never ill-treated any one. You complain that there is no love in this marriage. I prove that there is, and you become still more angry. What do you want? Do you suppose she will not be contented? Glad enough she is to get me, and she will do her duty well."

"Her duty!" cried Miss Abbott, with all the bitterness of which she was capable.

"Why, of course. She knows why I am marrying her."

"To succeed where Lilia failed! To be your housekeeper, your slave, you——" The words she would like to have said were too violent for her.

"To look after the baby, certainly," said he.

"The baby——?" She had forgotten it.

"It is an English marriage," he said proudly. "I do not care about the money. I am having her for my son. Did you not understand that?"

"No," said Miss Abbott, utterly bewildered. Then, for a moment, she saw light. "It is not necessary, Signor Carella. Since you are tired of the baby——"

Ever after she remembered it to her credit that she saw her mistake at once. "I don't mean that," she added quickly.

"I know," was his courteous response. "Ah, in a foreign language (and how perfectly you speak Italian) one is certain to make slips."

She looked at his face. It was apparently innocent of satire.

"You meant that we could not always be together yet, he and I. You are right. What is to be done? I cannot afford a nurse, and Perfetta is too rough. When he was ill I dare not let her touch him When he has to be washed, which happens now and then, who does it? I. I feed him, or settle what he shall have. I sleep with him and comfort him when he is unhappy in the night. No one talks, no one may sing to him but I. Do not be unfair this time; I like to do these things. But nevertheless (his voice became pathetic) they take up a great deal of time, and are not all suitable for a young man."

"Not at all suitable," said Miss Abbott, and closed her eyes wearily. Each moment her difficulties were increasing. She wished that she was not so tired, so open to contradictory impressions. She longed for Harriet's burly obtuseness or for the soulless diplomacy of Mrs. Herriton.

"A little more wine?" asked Gino kindly.

"Oh, no, thank you! But marriage, Signor Carella, is a very serious step. Could you not manage more simply? Your relative, for example——"

"Empoli! I would as soon have him in England!"

"England, then——"

He laughed.

"He has a grandmother there, you know—Mrs. Theobald."

"He has a grandmother here. No, he is troublesome, but I must have him with me. I will not even have my father and mother too. For they would separate us," he added.

"How?"

"They would separate our thoughts."

She was silent. This cruel, vicious fellow knew of strange refinements. The horrible truth, that wicked people are capable of love, stood naked before her, and her moral being was abashed. It was her duty to rescue the baby, to save it from contagion, and she still meant to do her duty. But the comfortable sense of virtue left her. She was in the presence of something greater than right or wrong.

Forgetting that this was an interview, he had strolled back into the room, driven by the instinct she had aroused in him. "Wake up!" he cried to his baby, as if it was some grown-up friend. Then he lifted his foot and trod lightly on its stomach.

Miss Abbott cried, "Oh, take care!" She was unaccustomed to this method of awakening the young.

"He is not much longer than my boot, is he? Can you believe that in time his own boots will be as large? And that he also——"

"But ought you to treat him like that?"

He stood with one foot resting on the little body, suddenly musing, filled with the desire that his son should be like him, and should have sons like him, to people the earth. It is the strongest desire that can come to a man—if it comes to him at all—stronger even than love or the desire for personal immortality. All men vaunt it, and declare that it is theirs; but the hearts of most are set elsewhere. It is the exception who comprehends that physical and spiritual life may stream out of him for ever. Miss Abbott, for all her goodness, could not comprehend it, though such a thing is more within the comprehension of women. And when Gino pointed first to himself and then to his baby and said "father—son," she still took it as a piece of nursery prattle, and smiled mechanically.

The child, the first fruits, woke up and glared at her. Gino did not greet it, but continued the exposition of his policy.

"This woman will do exactly what I tell her. She is fond of children. She is clean; she has a pleasant voice. She is not beautiful; I cannot pretend that to you for a moment. But she is what I require."

The baby gave a piercing yell.

"Oh, do take care!" begged Miss Abbott. "You are squeezing it."

"It is nothing. If he cries silently then you may be frightened. He thinks I am going to wash him, and he is quite right."

"Wash him!" she cried. "You? Here?" The homely piece of news seemed to shatter all her plans. She had spent a long half-hour in elaborate approaches, in high moral attacks; she had neither frightened her enemy nor made him angry, nor interfered with the least detail of his domestic life.

"I had gone to the Farmacia," he continued, "and was sitting there comfortably, when suddenly I remembered that Perfetta had heated water an hour ago—over there, look, covered with a cushion. I came away at once, for really he must be washed. You must excuse me. I can put it off no longer."

"I have wasted your time," she said feebly.

He walked sternly to the loggia and drew from it a large earthenware bowl. It was dirty inside; he dusted it with a tablecloth. Then he fetched the hot water, which was in a copper pot. He poured it out. He added cold. He felt in his pocket and brought out a piece of soap. Then he took up the baby, and, holding his cigar between his teeth, began to unwrap it. Miss Abbott turned to go.

"But why are you going? Excuse me if I wash him while we talk."

"I have nothing more to say," said Miss Abbott. All she could do now was to find Philip, confess her miserable defeat, and bid him go in her stead and prosper better. She cursed her feebleness; she longed to expose it, without apologies or tears.

"Oh, but stop a moment!" he cried. "You have not seen him yet."

"I have seen as much as I want, thank you."

The last wrapping slid off. He held out to her in his two hands a little kicking image of bronze.

"Take him!"

She would not touch the child.

"I must go at once," she cried; for the tears—the wrong tears—were hurrying to her eyes.

"Who would have believed his mother was blonde? For he is brown all over—brown every inch of him. Ah, but how beautiful he is! And he is mine; mine for ever. Even if he hates me he will be mine. He cannot help it; he is made out of me; I am his father."

It was too late to go. She could not tell why, but it was too late. She turned away her head when Gino lifted his son to his lips. This was something too remote from the prettiness of the nursery. The man was majestic; he was a part of Nature; in no ordinary love scene could he ever be so great. For a wonderful physical tie binds the parents to the children; and—by some sad, strange irony—it does not bind us children to our parents. For if it did, if we could answer their love not with gratitude but with equal love, life would lose much of its pathos and much of its squalor, and we might be wonderfully happy. Gino passionately embracing, Miss Abbott reverently averting her eyes—both of them had parents whom they did not love so very much.

"May I help you to wash him?" she asked humbly.

He gave her his son without speaking, and they knelt side by side, tucking up their sleeves. The child had stopped crying, and his arms and legs were agitated by some overpowering joy. Miss Abbott had a woman's pleasure in cleaning anything—more especially when the thing was human. She understood little babies from long experience in a district, and Gino soon ceased to give her directions, and only gave her thanks.

"It is very kind of you," he murmured, "especially in your beautiful dress. He is nearly clean already. Why, I take the whole morning! There is so much more of a baby than one expects. And Perfetta washes him just as she washes clothes. Then he screams for hours. My wife is to have a light hand. Ah, how he kicks! Has he splashed you? I am very sorry."

"I am ready for a soft towel now," said Miss Abbott, who was strangely exalted by the service.

"Certainly! certainly!" He strode in a knowing way to a cupboard. But he had no idea where the soft towel was. Generally he dabbed the baby on the first dry thing he found.

"And if you had any powder."

He struck his forehead despairingly. Apparently the stock of powder was just exhausted.

She sacrificed her own clean handkerchief. He put a chair for her on the loggia, which faced westward, and was still pleasant and cool. There she sat, with twenty miles of view behind her, and he placed the dripping baby on her knee. It shone now with health and beauty: it seemed to reflect light, like a copper vessel. Just such a baby Bellini sets languid on his mother's lap, or Signorelli flings wriggling on pavements of marble, or Lorenzo di Credi, more reverent but less divine, lays carefully among flowers, with his head upon a wisp of golden straw. For a time Gino contemplated them standing. Then, to get a better view, he knelt by the side of the chair, with his hands clasped before him.

So they were when Philip entered, and saw, to all intents and purposes, the Virgin and Child, with Donor.

"Hullo!" he exclaimed; for he was glad to find things in such cheerful trim.

She did not greet him, but rose up unsteadily and handed the baby to his father.

"No, do stop!" whispered Philip. "I got your note. I'm not offended; you're quite right. I really want you; I could never have done it alone."

No words came from her, but she raised her hands to her mouth, like one who is in sudden agony.

"Signorina, do stop a little—after all your kindness."

She burst into tears.

"What is it?" said Philip kindly.

She tried to speak, and then went away weeping bitterly.

The two men stared at each other. By a common impulse they ran on to the loggia. They were just in time to see Miss Abbott disappear among the trees.

"What is it?" asked Philip again. There was no answer, and somehow he did not want an answer. Some strange thing had happened which he could not presume to understand. He would find out from Miss Abbott, if ever he found out at all.

"Well, your business," said Gino, after a puzzled sigh.

"Our business—Miss Abbott has told you of that."

"No."

"But surely——"

"She came for business. But she forgot about it; so did I."

Perfetta, who had a genius for missing people, now returned, loudly complaining of the size of Monteriano and the intricacies of its streets. Gino told her to watch the baby. Then he offered Philip a cigar, and they proceeded to the business.

Chapter Eight

"MAD!" SCREAMED HARRIET, —"absolutely stark, staring, raving mad!"

Philip judged it better not to contradict her.

"What's she here for? Answer me that. What's she doing in Monteriano in August? Why isn't she in Normandy? Answer that. She won't. I can: she's come to thwart us; she's betrayed us—got hold of mother's plans. Oh, goodness, my head!"

He was unwise enough to reply, "You mustn't accuse her of that. Though she is exasperating, she hasn't come here to betray us."

"Then why has she come here? Answer me that."

He made no answer. But fortunately his sister was too much agitated to wait for one. "Bursting in on me—crying and looking a disgusting sight—and says she has been to see the Italian. Couldn't even talk properly; pretended she had changed her opinions. What are her opinions to us? I was very calm. I said: 'Miss Abbott, I think there is a little misapprehension in this matter. My mother, Mrs. Herriton——' Oh, goodness, my head! Of course you've failed—don't trouble to answer—I know you've failed. Where's the baby, pray? Of course you haven't got it. Dear sweet Caroline won't let you. Oh, yes, and we're to go away at once and trouble the father no more. Those are her commands. Commands! COMMANDS!" And Harriet also burst into tears.

Philip governed his temper. His sister was annoying, but quite reasonable in her indignation. Moreover, Miss Abbott had behaved even worse than she supposed.

"I've not got the baby, Harriet, but at the same time I haven't exactly failed. I and Signor Carella are to have another interview this afternoon, at the Caffè Garibaldi. He is perfectly reasonable and pleasant. Should you be disposed to come with me, you would find him quite willing to discuss things. He is desperately in want of money, and has no prospect of getting any. I discovered that. At the same time, he has a certain affection for the child." For Philip's insight, or perhaps his opportunities, had not been equal to Miss Abbott's.

Harriet would only sob, and accuse her brother of insulting her; how could a lady speak to such a horrible man? That, and nothing else, was enough to stamp Caroline. Oh, poor Lilia!

Philip drummed on the bedroom window-sill. He saw no escape from the deadlock. For though he spoke cheerfully about his second interview with Gino, he felt at the bottom of his heart that it would fail. Gino was too courteous: he would not break off negotiations by sharp denial; he loved this civil, half-humorous bargaining. And he loved fooling his opponent, and did it so nicely that his opponent did not mind being fooled.

"Miss Abbott has behaved extraordinarily," he said at last; "but at the same time——"

His sister would not hear him. She burst forth again on the madness, the interference, the intolerable duplicity of Caroline.

"Harriet, you must listen. My dear, you must stop crying. I have something quite important to say."

"I shall not stop crying," said she. But in time, finding that he would not speak to her, she did stop.

"Remember that Miss Abbott has done us no harm. She said nothing to him about the matter. He assumes that she is working with us: I gathered that."

"Well, she isn't."

"Yes; but if you're careful she may be. I interpret her behaviour thus: She went to see him, honestly intending to get the child away. In the note she left me she says so, and I don't believe she'd lie."

"I do."

"When she got there, there was some pretty domestic scene between him and the baby, and she has got swept off in a gush of sentimentalism. Before very long, if I know anything about psychology, there will be a reaction. She'll be swept back."

"I don't understand your long words. Say plainly——"

"When she's swept back, she'll be invaluable. For she has made quite an impression on him. He thinks her so nice with the baby. You know, she washed it for him."

"Disgusting!"

Harriet's ejaculations were more aggravating than the rest of her. But Philip was averse to losing his temper. The access of joy that had come to him yesterday in the theatre promised to be permanent. He was more anxious than heretofore to be charitable towards the world.

"If you want to carry off the baby, keep your peace with Miss Abbott. For if she chooses, she can help you better than I can."

"There can be no peace between me and her," said Harriet gloomily.

"Did you——"

"Oh, not all I wanted. She went away before I had finished speaking—just like those cowardly people!—into the church."

"Into Santa Deodata's?"

"Yes; I'm sure she needs it. Anything more unchristian——"

In time Philip went to the church also, leaving his sister a little calmer and a little disposed to think over his advice. What had come over Miss Abbott? He had always thought her both stable and sincere. That conversation he had had with her last Christmas in the train to Charing Cross—that alone furnished him with a parallel. For the second time, Monteriano must have turned her head. He was not angry with her, for he was quite indifferent to the outcome of their expedition. He was only extremely interested.

It was now nearly midday, and the streets were clearing. But the intense heat had broken, and there was a pleasant suggestion of rain. The Piazza, with its three great attractions—the Palazzo Pubblico, the Collegiate Church, and the Caffè Garibaldi: the intellect, the soul, and the body—had never looked more charming. For a moment Philip stood in its centre, much inclined to be dreamy, and thinking how wonderful it must feel to belong to a city, however mean. He was here, however, as an emissary of civilization and as a student of character, and, after a sigh, he entered Santa Deodata's to continue his mission.

There had been a *festa* two days before, and the church still smelt of incense and of garlic. The little son of the sacristan was sweeping the nave, more for amusement than for cleanliness, sending great clouds of dust over the frescoes and the scattered worshippers. The sacristan himself had propped a ladder in the centre of the Deluge—which fills one of the nave spandrels—and was freeing a column from its wealth of scarlet calico. Much scarlet calico also lay upon the floor—for the church can look as fine as any theatre—and the sacristan's little daughter was trying to fold it up. She was wearing a tinsel crown. The crown really belonged to St. Augustine. But it had been cut too big: it fell down over his cheeks like a collar: you never saw anything so absurd. One of the canons had unhooked it just before the *fiesta* began, and had given it to the sacristan's daughter.

"Please," cried Philip, "is there an English lady here?"

The man's mouth was full of tin-tacks, but he nodded cheerfully towards a kneeling figure. In the midst of this confusion Miss Abbott was praying.

He was not much surprised: a spiritual breakdown was quite to be expected. For though he was growing more charitable towards mankind, he was still a little jaunty, and too apt to stake out beforehand the course that will be pursued by the wounded soul. It did not surprise him, however, that she should greet him naturally, with none of the sour self-consciousness of a person who had just risen from her knees. This was indeed the spirit of Santa Deodata's, where a prayer to God is thought none the worse of because it comes next to a pleasant word to a neighbour. "I am sure that I need it," said she; and he, who had expected her to be ashamed, became confused, and knew not what to reply.

"I've nothing to tell you," she continued. "I have simply changed straight round. If I had planned the whole thing out, I could not have treated you worse. I can talk it over now; but please believe that I have been crying."

"And please believe that I have not come to scold you," said Philip. "I know what has happened."

"What?" asked Miss Abbott. Instinctively she led the way to the famous chapel, the fifth chapel on the right, wherein Giovanni da Empoli has painted the death and burial of the saint. Here they could sit out of the dust and the noise, and proceed with a discussion which promised to be important.

"What might have happened to me—he had made you believe that he loved the child."

"Oh, yes; he has. He will never give it up."

"At present it is still unsettled."

"It will never be settled."

"Perhaps not. Well, as I said, I know what has happened, and I am not here to scold you. But I must ask you to withdraw from the thing for the present. Harriet is furious. But she will calm down when she realizes that you have done us no harm, and will do none."

"I can do no more," she said. "But I tell you plainly I have changed sides."

"If you do no more, that is all we want. You promise not to prejudice our cause by speaking to Signor Carella?"

"Oh, certainly. I don't want to speak to him again; I shan't ever see him again."

"Quite nice, wasn't he?"

"Quite."

"Well, that's all I wanted to know. I'll go and tell Harriet of your promise, and I think things'll quiet down now."

But he did not move, for it was an increasing pleasure to him to be near her, and her charm was at its strongest today. He thought less of psychology and feminine reaction. The gush of sentimentalism which had carried her away had only made her more alluring. He was content to observe her beauty and to profit by the tenderness and the wisdom that dwelt within her.

"Why aren't you angry with me?" she asked, after a pause.

"Because I understand you—all sides, I think,—Harriet, Signor Carella, even my mother."

"You do understand wonderfully. You are the only one of us who has a general view of the muddle."

He smiled with pleasure. It was the first time she had ever praised him. His eyes rested agreeably on Santa Deodata, who was dying in full sanctity, upon her back. There was a window open behind her, revealing just such a view as he had seen that morning, and on her widowed mother's dresser there stood just such another copper pot The saint looked neither at the view nor at the pot, and at her widowed mother still less. For lo! she had a vision: the head and shoulders of St. Augustine were sliding like some miraculous enamel along the rough-cast wall. It is a gentle saint who is content with half another saint to see her die. In her death, as in her life, Santa Deodata did not accomplish much.

"So what are you going to do?" said Miss Abbott.

Philip started, not so much at the words as at the sudden change in the voice. "Do?" he echoed, rather dismayed. "This afternoon I have another interview."

"It will come to nothing. Well?"

"Then another. If that fails I shall wire home for instructions. I dare say we may fail altogether, but we shall fail honourably."

She had often been decided. But now behind her decision there was a note of passion. She struck him not as different, but as more important, and he minded it very much when she said—

"That's not doing anything! You would be doing something if you kidnapped the baby, or if you went straight away. But that! To fail honourably! To come out of the thing as well as you can! Is that all you are after?"

"Why, yes," he stammered. "Since we talk openly, that is all I am after just now. What else is there? If I can persuade Signor Carella to give in, so much the better. If he won't, I must report the failure to my mother and then go home. Why, Miss Abbott, you can't expect me to follow you through all these turns——"

"I don't! But I do expect you to settle what is right and to follow that. Do you want the child to stop with his father, who loves him and will bring him up badly, or do you want him to come to Sawston, where no one loves him, but where he will be brought up well? There is the question put dispassionately enough even for you. Settle it. Settle which side you'll fight on. But don't go talking about an 'honourable failure,' which means simply not thinking and not acting at all."

"Because I understand the position of Signor Carella and of you, it's no reason that——"

"None at all. Fight as if you think us wrong. Oh, what's the use of your fair-mindedness if you never decide for yourself? Any one gets hold of you and makes you do what they want. And you see through them and laugh at them—and do it. It's not enough to see clearly; I'm muddle-headed and stupid, and not worth a quarter of you, but I have tried to do what seemed right at the time. And you—your brain and your insight are splendid. But when you see what's right you're too idle to do it. You told me once that we shall be judged by our intentions, not by our accomplishments. I thought it a grand remark. But we must intend to accomplish—not sit intending on a chair."

"You are wonderful!" he said gravely.

"Oh, you appreciate me!" she burst out again. "I wish you didn't. You appreciate us all—see good in all of us. And all the time you are dead—dead—

dead. Look, why aren't you angry?" She came up to him, and then her mood suddenly changed, and she took hold of both his hands. "You are so splendid, Mr. Herriton, that I can't bear to see you wasted. I can't bear—she has not been good to you—your mother."

"Miss Abbott, don't worry over me. Some people are born not to do things. I'm one of them; I never did anything at school or at the Bar. I came out to stop Lilia's marriage, and it was too late. I came out intending to get the baby, and I shall return an 'honourable failure.' I never expect anything to happen now, and so I am never disappointed. You would be surprised to know what my great events are. Going to the theatre yesterday, talking to you now— I don't suppose I shall ever meet anything greater. I seem fated to pass through the world without colliding with it or moving it—and I'm sure I can't tell you whether the fate's good or evil. I don't die—I don't fall in love. And if other people die or fall in love they always do it when I'm just not there. You are quite right; life to me is just a spectacle, which— thank God, and thank Italy, and thank you—is now more beautiful and heartening than it has ever been before."

She said solemnly, "I wish something would happen to you, my dear friend; I wish something would happen to you."

"But why?" he asked, smiling. "Prove to me why I don't do as I am."

She also smiled, very gravely. She could not prove it. No argument existed. Their discourse, splendid as it had been, resulted in nothing, and their respective opinions and policies were exactly the same when they left the church as when they had entered it.

Harriet was rude at lunch. She called Miss Abbott a turncoat and a coward to her face. Miss Abbott resented neither epithet, feeling that one was justified and the other not unreasonable. She tried to avoid even the suspicion of satire in her replies. But Harriet was sure that she was satirical because she was so calm. She got more and more violent, and Philip at one time feared that she would come to blows.

"Look here!" he cried, with something of the old manner, "it's too hot for this. We've been talking and interviewing each other all the morning, and I have another interview this afternoon. I do stipulate for silence. Let each lady retire to her bedroom with a book."

"I retire to pack," said Harriet. "Please remind Signor Carella, Philip, that the baby is to be here by half-past eight this evening."

"Oh, certainly, Harriet. I shall make a point of reminding him."

"And order a carriage to take us to the evening train."

"And please," said Miss Abbott, "would you order a carriage for me too?"

"You going?" he exclaimed.

"Of course," she replied, suddenly flushing. "Why not?"

"Why, of course you would be going. Two carriages, then. Two carriages for the evening train." He looked at his sister hopelessly. "Harriet, whatever are you up to? We shall never be ready."

"Order my carriage for the evening train," said Harriet, and departed.

"Well, I suppose I shall. And I shall also have my interview with Signor Carella."

Miss Abbott gave a little sigh.

"But why should you mind? Do you suppose that I shall have the slightest influence over him?"

"No. But—I can't repeat all that I said in the church. You ought never to see him again. You ought to bundle Harriet into a carriage, not this evening, but now, and drive her straight away."

"Perhaps I ought. But it isn't a very big 'ought.' Whatever Harriet and I do the issue is the same. Why, I can see the splendour of it—even the humour. Gino sitting up here on the mountain-top with his cub. We come and ask for it. He welcomes us. We ask for it again. He is equally pleasant. I'm agreeable to spend the whole week bargaining with him. But I know that at the end of it I shall descend empty-handed to the plains. It might be finer of me to make up my mind. But I'm not a fine character. And nothing hangs on it."

"Perhaps I am extreme," she said humbly. "I've been trying to run you, just like your mother. I feel you ought to fight it out with Harriet. Every little trifle, for some reason, does seem incalculably important today, and when you say of a thing that 'nothing hangs on it,' it sounds like blasphemy. There's never any knowing—(how am I to put it?)—which of our actions, which of our idlenesses won't have things hanging on it for ever."

He assented, but her remark had only an aesthetic value. He was not prepared to take it to his heart. All the afternoon he rested—worried, but not exactly despondent. The thing would jog out somehow. Probably Miss Abbott was right. The baby had better stop where it was loved. And that, probably, was what the fates had decreed. He felt little interest in the matter, and he was sure that he had no influence.

It was not surprising, therefore, that the interview at the Caffè Garibaldi came to nothing. Neither of them took it very seriously. And before long Gino had discovered how things lay, and was ragging his companion hopelessly. Philip tried to look offended, but in the end he had to laugh. "Well, you are right," he said. "This affair is being managed by the ladies."

"Ah, the ladies—the ladies!" cried the other, and then he roared like a millionaire for two cups of black coffee, and insisted on treating his friend, as a sign that their strife was over.

"Well, I have done my best," said Philip, dipping a long slice of sugar into his cup, and watching the brown liquid ascend into it. "I shall face my mother with a good conscience. Will you bear me witness that I've done my best?"

"My poor fellow, I will!" He laid a sympathetic hand on Philip's knee.

"And that I have——" The sugar was now impregnated with coffee, and he bent forward to swallow it. As he did so his eyes swept the opposite of the Piazza, and he saw there, watching them, Harriet. "Mia sorella!" he exclaimed. Gino, much amused, laid his hand upon the little table, and beat the marble humorously with his fists. Harriet turned away and began gloomily to inspect the Palazzo Pubblico.

"Poor Harriet!" said Philip, swallowing the sugar. "One more wrench and it will all be over for her; we are leaving this evening."

Gino was sorry for this. "Then you will not be here this evening as you promised us. All three leaving?"

"All three," said Philip, who had not revealed the secession of Miss Abbott; "by the night train; at least, that is my sister's plan. So I'm afraid I shan't be here."

They watched the departing figure of Harriet, and then entered upon the final civilities. They shook each other warmly by both hands. Philip was to come again next year, and to write beforehand. He was to be introduced to Gino's wife, for he was told of the marriage now. He was to be godfather to his next baby. As for Gino, he would remember some time that Philip liked vermouth. He begged him to give his love to Irma. Mrs. Herriton—should he send her his sympathetic regards? No; perhaps that would hardly do.

So the two young men parted with a good deal of genuine affection. For the barrier of language is sometimes a blessed barrier, which only lets pass what is good. Or—to put the thing less cynically—we may be better in new clean words, which have never been tainted by our pettiness or vice. Philip, at all events, lived more graciously in Italian, the very phrases of which entice one to be happy and kind. It was horrible to think of the English of Harriet, whose every word would be as hard, as distinct, and as unfinished as a lump of coal.

Harriet, however, talked little. She had seen enough to know that her brother had failed again, and with unwonted dignity she accepted the situation. She did her packing, she wrote up her diary, she made a brown paper cover for the new Baedeker. Philip, finding her so amenable, tried to discuss their future plans. But she only said that they would sleep in Florence, and told him to telegraph for rooms. They had supper alone. Miss Abbott did not come down. The landlady told them that Signor Carella had called on Miss Abbott to say good-bye, but she, though in, had not been able to see him. She also told them that it had begun to rain. Harriet sighed, but indicated to her brother that he was not responsible.

The carriages came round at a quarter past eight. It was not raining much, but the night was extraordinarily dark, and one of the drivers wanted to go slowly to the station. Miss Abbott came down and said that she was ready, and would start at once.

"Yes, do," said Philip, who was standing in the hall. "Now that we have quarrelled we scarcely want to travel in procession all the way down the hill. Well, good-bye; it's all over at last; another scene in my pageant has shifted."

"Good-bye; it's been a great pleasure to see you. I hope that won't shift, at all events." She gripped his hand.

"You sound despondent," he said, laughing. "Don't forget that you return victorious."

"I suppose I do," she replied, more despondently than ever, and got into the carriage. He concluded that she was thinking of her reception at Sawston, whither her fame would doubtless precede her. Whatever would Mrs. Herriton do? She could make things quite unpleasant when she thought it right. She might think it right to be silent, but then there was Harriet. Who would bridle Harriet's tongue? Between the two of them Miss Abbott was bound to have a bad time. Her reputation, both for consistency and for moral enthusiasm, would be lost for ever.

"It's hard luck on her," he thought. "She is a good person. I must do for her anything I can." Their intimacy had been very rapid, but he too hoped that it would not shift. He believed that he understood her, and that she, by now, had seen the worst of him. What if after a long time—if after all—he flushed like a boy as he looked after her carriage.

He went into the dining-room to look for Harriet. Harriet was not to be found. Her bedroom, too, was empty. All that was left of her was the purple prayer-book which lay open on the bed. Philip took it up aimlessly, and saw—"Blessed be the Lord my God who teacheth my hands to war and my fingers to fight." He put the book in his pocket, and began to brood over more profitable themes.

Santa Deodata gave out half past eight. All the luggage was on, and still Harriet had not appeared. "Depend upon it," said the landlady, "she has gone to Signor Carella's to say good-bye to her little nephew." Philip did not think it likely. They shouted all over the house and still there was no Harriet. He began to be uneasy. He was helpless without Miss Abbott; her grave, kind face had cheered him wonderfully, even when it looked displeased. Monteriano was sad without her; the rain was thickening; the scraps of

Donizetti floated tunelessly out of the wineshops, and of the great tower opposite he could only see the base, fresh papered with the advertisements of quacks.

A man came up the street with a note. Philip read, "Start at once. Pick me up outside the gate. Pay the bearer. H. H."

"Did the lady give you this note?" he cried.

The man was unintelligible.

"Speak up!" exclaimed Philip. "Who gave it you—and where?"

Nothing but horrible sighings and bubblings came out of the man.

"Be patient with him," said the driver, turning round on the box. "It is the poor idiot." And the landlady came out of the hotel and echoed "The poor idiot. He cannot speak. He takes messages for us all."

Philip then saw that the messenger was a ghastly creature, quite bald, with trickling eyes and grey twitching nose. In another country he would have been shut up; here he was accepted as a public institution, and part of Nature's scheme.

"Ugh!" shuddered the Englishman. "Signora padrona, find out from him; this note is from my sister. What does it mean? Where did he see her?"

"It is no good," said the landlady. "He understands everything but he can explain nothing."

"He has visions of the saints," said the man who drove the cab.

"But my sister—where has she gone? How has she met him?"

"She has gone for a walk," asserted the landlady. It was a nasty evening, but she was beginning to understand the English. "She has gone for a walk—perhaps to wish good-bye to her little nephew. Preferring to come back another way, she has sent you this note by the poor idiot and is waiting for you outside the Siena gate. Many of my guests do this."

There was nothing to do but to obey the message. He shook hands with the landlady, gave the messenger a nickel piece, and drove away. After a dozen yards the carriage stopped. The poor idiot was running and whimpering behind.

"Go on," cried Philip. "I have paid him plenty."

A horrible hand pushed three soldi into his lap. It was part of the idiot's malady only to receive what was just for his services. This was the change out of the nickel piece.

"Go on!" shouted Philip, and flung the money into the road. He was frightened at the episode; the whole of life had become unreal. It was a relief to be out of the Siena gate. They drew up for a moment on the terrace. But there was no sign of Harriet. The driver called to the Dogana men. But they had seen no English lady pass.

"What am I to do?" he cried; "it is not like the lady to be late. We shall miss the train."

"Let us drive slowly," said the driver, "and you shall call her by name as we go."

So they started down into the night, Philip calling "Harriet! Harriet! Harriet!" And there she was, waiting for them in the wet, at the first turn of the zigzag.

"Harriet, why don't you answer?"

"I heard you coming," said she, and got quickly in. Not till then did he see that she carried a bundle.

"What's that?"

"Hush——"

"Whatever is that?"

"Hush—sleeping."

Harriet had succeeded where Miss Abbott and Philip had failed. It was the baby.

She would not let him talk. The baby, she repeated, was asleep, and she put up an umbrella to shield it and her from the rain. He should hear all later, so he had to conjecture the course of the wonderful interview—an interview between the South pole and the North. It was quite easy to conjecture: Gino crumpling up suddenly before the intense conviction of Harriet; being told, perhaps, to his face that he was a villain; yielding his only son perhaps for money, perhaps for nothing. "Poor Gino," he thought. "He's no greater than I am, after all."

Then he thought of Miss Abbott, whose carriage must be descending the darkness some mile or two below them, and his easy self-accusation failed. She, too, had conviction; he had felt its force; he would feel it again when she knew this day's sombre and unexpected close.

"You have been pretty secret," he said; "you might tell me a little now. What do we pay for him? All we've got?"

"Hush!" answered Harriet, and dandled the bundle laboriously, like some bony prophetess— Judith, or Deborah, or Jael. He had last seen the baby sprawling on the knees of Miss Abbott, shining and naked, with twenty miles of view behind him, and his father kneeling by his feet. And that remembrance, together with Harriet, and the darkness, and the poor idiot, and the silent rain, filled him with sorrow and with the expectation of sorrow to come.

Monteriano had long disappeared, and he could see nothing but the occasional wet stem of an olive, which their lamp illumined as they passed it. They travelled quickly, for this driver did not care how fast he went to the station, and would dash down each incline and scuttle perilously round the curves.

"Look here, Harriet," he said at last, "I feel bad; I want to see the baby."

"Hush!"

"I don't mind if I do wake him up. I want to see him. I've as much right in him as you."

Harriet gave in. But it was too dark for him to see the child's face. "Wait a minute," he whispered, and before she could stop him he had lit a match under the shelter of her umbrella. "But he's awake!" he exclaimed. The match went out.

"Good ickle quiet boysey, then."

Philip winced. "His face, do you know, struck me as all wrong."

"All wrong?"

"All puckered queerly."

"Of course—with the shadows—you couldn't see him."

"Well, hold him up again." She did so. He lit another match. It went out quickly, but not before he had seen that the baby was crying.

"Nonsense," said Harriet sharply. "We should hear him if he cried."

"No, he's crying hard; I thought so before, and I'm certain now."

Harriet touched the child's face. It was bathed in

tears. "Oh, the night air, I suppose," she said, "or perhaps the wet of the rain."

"I say, you haven't hurt it, or held it the wrong way, or anything; it is too uncanny—crying and no noise. Why didn't you get Perfetta to carry it to the hotel instead of muddling with the messenger? It's a marvel he understood about the note."

"Oh, he understands." And he could feel her shudder. "He tried to carry the baby——"

"But why not Gino or Perfetta?"

"Philip, don't talk. Must I say it again? Don't talk. The baby wants to sleep." She crooned harshly as they descended, and now and then she wiped up the tears which welled inexhaustibly from the little eyes. Philip looked away, winking at times himself. It was as if they were travelling with the whole world's sorrow, as if all the mystery, all the persistency of woe were gathered to a single fount. The roads were now coated with mud, and the carriage went more quietly but not less swiftly, sliding by long zigzags into the night. He knew the landmarks pretty well: here was the crossroad to Poggibonsi; and the last view of Monteriano, if they had light, would be from here. Soon they ought to come to that little wood where violets were so plentiful in spring. He wished the weather had not changed; it was not cold, but the air was extraordinarily damp. It could not be good for the child.

"I suppose he breathes, and all that sort of thing?" he said.

"Of course," said Harriet, in an angry whisper. "You've started him again. I'm certain he was asleep.

I do wish you wouldn't talk; it makes me so nervous."

"I'm nervous too. I wish he'd scream. It's too uncanny. Poor Gino! I'm terribly sorry for Gino."

"Are you?"

"Because he's weak—like most of us. He doesn't know what he wants. He doesn't grip on to life. But I like that man, and I'm sorry for him."

Naturally enough she made no answer.

"You despise him, Harriet, and you despise me. But you do us no good by it. We fools want some one to set us on our feet. Suppose a really decent woman had set up Gino—I believe Caroline Abbott might have done it—mightn't he have been another man?"

"Philip," she interrupted, with an attempt at nonchalance, "do you happen to have those matches handy? We might as well look at the baby again if you have."

The first match blew out immediately. So did the second. He suggested that they should stop the carriage and borrow the lamp from the driver.

"Oh, I don't want all that bother. Try again."

They entered the little wood as he tried to strike the third match. At last it caught. Harriet poised the umbrella rightly, and for a full quarter minute they contemplated the face that trembled in the light of the trembling flame. Then there was a shout and a crash. They were lying in the mud in darkness. The carriage had overturned.

Philip was a good deal hurt. He sat up and rocked himself to and fro, holding his arm. He could just make out the outline of the carriage above him, and the outlines of the carriage cushions and of their luggage upon the grey road. The accident had taken place in the wood, where it was even darker than in the open.

"Are you all right?" he managed to say. Harriet was screaming, the horse was kicking, the driver was cursing some other man.

Harriet's screams became coherent. "The baby—the baby—it slipped—it's gone from my arms—I stole it!"

"God help me!" said Philip. A cold circle came round his mouth, and he fainted.

When he recovered it was still the same confusion. The horse was kicking, the baby had not been found, and Harriet still screamed like a maniac, "I stole it! I stole it! I stole it! It slipped out of my arms!"

"Keep still!" he commanded the driver. "Let no one move. We may tread on it. Keep still."

For a moment they all obeyed him. He began to crawl through the mud, touching first this, then that, grasping the cushions by mistake, listening for the faintest whisper that might guide him. He tried to light a match, holding the box in his teeth and striking at it with the uninjured hand. At last he succeeded, and the light fell upon the bundle which he was seeking.

It had rolled off the road into the wood a little way, and had fallen across a great rut. So tiny it was that had it fallen lengthways it would have disappeared, and he might never have found it.

"I stole it! I and the idiot—no one was there." She burst out laughing.

He sat down and laid it on his knee. Then he tried to cleanse the face from the mud and the rain and the tears. His arm, he supposed, was broken, but he could still move it a little, and for the moment he forgot all pain. He was listening—not for a cry, but for the tick of a heart or the slightest tremor of breath.

"Where are you?" called a voice. It was Miss Abbott, against whose carriage they had collided. She had relit one of the lamps, and was picking her way towards him.

"Silence!" he called again, and again they obeyed. He shook the bundle; he breathed into it; he opened his coat and pressed it against him. Then he listened, and heard nothing but the rain and the panting horses, and Harriet, who was somewhere chuckling to herself in the dark.

Miss Abbott approached, and took it gently from him. The face was already chilly, but thanks to Philip it was no longer wet. Nor would it again be wetted by any tear.

Chapter Nine

THE DETAILS OF Harriet's crime were never known. In her illness she spoke more of the inlaid box that she lent to Lilia—lent, not given—than of recent troubles. It was clear that she had gone prepared for an interview with Gino, and finding him out, she had yielded to a grotesque temptation. But how far this was the result of ill-temper, to what extent she had been fortified by her religion, when and how she had met the poor idiot—these questions were never answered, nor did they interest Philip greatly. Detection was certain: they would have been arrested by the police of Florence or Milan, or at the frontier. As it was, they had been stopped in a simpler manner a few miles out of the town.

As yet he could scarcely survey the thing. It was too great. Round the Italian baby who had died in the mud there centred deep passions and high hopes.

People had been wicked or wrong in the matter; no one save himself had been trivial. Now the baby had gone, but there remained this vast apparatus of pride and pity and love. For the dead, who seemed to take away so much, really take with them nothing that is ours. The passion they have aroused lives after them, easy to transmute or to transfer, but well-nigh impossible to destroy. And Philip knew that he was still voyaging on the same magnificent, perilous sea, with the sun or the clouds above him, and the tides below.

The course of the moment—that, at all events, was certain. He and no one else must take the news to Gino. It was easy to talk of Harriet's crime—easy also to blame the negligent Perfetta or Mrs. Herriton at home. Every one had contributed—even Miss Abbott and Irma. If one chose, one might consider the catastrophe composite or the work of fate. But Philip did not so choose. It was his own fault, due to acknowledged weakness in his own character. Therefore he, and no one else, must take the news of it to Gino.

Nothing prevented him. Miss Abbott was engaged with Harriet, and people had sprung out of the darkness and were conducting them towards some cottage. Philip had only to get into the uninjured carriage and order the driver to return. He was back at Monteriano after a two hours' absence. Perfetta was in the house now, and greeted him cheerfully. Pain, physical and mental, had made him stupid. It was some time before he realized that she had never missed the child.

Gino was still out. The woman took him to the reception-room, just as she had taken Miss Abbott in the morning, and dusted a circle for him on one of the horsehair chairs. But it was dark now, so she left the guest a little lamp.

"I will be as quick as I can," she told him. "But there are many streets in Monteriano; he is sometimes difficult to find. I could not find him this morning."

"Go first to the Caffè Garibaldi," said Philip, remembering that this was the hour appointed by his friends of yesterday.

He occupied the time he was left alone not in thinking—there was nothing to think about; he simply had to tell a few facts—but in trying to make a sling for his broken arm. The trouble was in the elbow-joint, and as long as he kept this motionless he could go on as usual. But inflammation was beginning, and the slightest jar gave him agony. The sling was not fitted before Gino leapt up the stairs, crying—

"So you are back! How glad I am! We are all waiting——"

Philip had seen too much to be nervous. In low, even tones he told what had happened; and the other, also perfectly calm, heard him to the end. In the silence Perfetta called up that she had forgotten the baby's evening milk; she must fetch it. When she had gone Gino took up the lamp without a word, and they went into the other room.

"My sister is ill," said Philip, "and Miss Abbott is guiltless. I should be glad if you did not have to trouble them."

Gino had stooped down by the way, and was

feeling the place where his son had lain. Now and then he frowned a little and glanced at Philip.

"It is through me," he continued. "It happened because I was cowardly and idle. I have come to know what you will do."

Gino had left the rug, and began to pat the table from the end, as if he was blind. The action was so uncanny that Philip was driven to intervene.

"Gently, man, gently; he is not here."

He went up and touched him on the shoulder.

He twitched away, and began to pass his hands over things more rapidly—over the table, the chairs, the entire floor, the walls as high as he could reach them. Philip had not presumed to comfort him. But now the tension was too great—he tried.

"Break down, Gino; you must break down. Scream and curse and give in for a little; you must break down."

There was no reply, and no cessation of the sweeping hands.

"It is time to be unhappy. Break down or you will be ill like my sister. You will go——"

The tour of the room was over. He had touched everything in it except Philip. Now he approached him. His face was that of a man who has lost his old reason for life and seeks a new one.

"Gino!"

He stopped for a moment; then he came nearer. Philip stood his ground.

"You are to do what you like with me, Gino. Your son is dead, Gino. He died in my arms, remember. It does not excuse me; but he did die in my arms."

The left hand came forward, slowly this time. It hovered before Philip like an insect. Then it descended and gripped him by his broken elbow.

Philip struck out with all the strength of his other arm. Gino fell to the blow without a cry or a word.

"You brute!" exclaimed the Englishman. "Kill me if you like! But just you leave my broken arm alone."

Then he was seized with remorse, and knelt beside his adversary and tried to revive him. He managed to raise him up, and propped his body against his own. He passed his arm round him. Again he was filled with pity and tenderness. He awaited the revival without fear, sure that both of them were safe at last.

Gino recovered suddenly. His lips moved. For one blessed moment it seemed that he was going to speak. But he scrambled up in silence, remembering everything, and he made not towards Philip, but towards the lamp.

"Do what you like; but think first——"

The lamp was tossed across the room, out through the loggia. It broke against one of the trees below. Philip began to cry out in the dark.

Gino approached from behind and gave him a sharp pinch. Philip spun round with a yell. He had only been pinched on the back, but he knew what was in store for him. He struck out, exhorting the devil to fight him, to kill him, to do anything but this. Then he stumbled to the door. It was open. He lost his head, and, instead of turning down the stairs, he ran across the landing into the room opposite.

There he lay down on the floor between the stove and the skirting-board.

His senses grew sharper. He could hear Gino coming in on tiptoe. He even knew what was passing in his mind, how now he was at fault, now he was hopeful, now he was wondering whether after all the victim had not escaped down the stairs. There was a quick swoop above him, and then a low growl like a dog's. Gino had broken his finger-nails against the stove.

Physical pain is almost too terrible to bear. We can just bear it when it comes by accident or for our good—as it generally does in modern life—except at school. But when it is caused by the malignity of a man, full grown, fashioned like ourselves, all our control disappears. Philip's one thought was to get away from that room at whatever sacrifice of nobility or pride.

Gino was now at the further end of the room, groping by the little tables. Suddenly the instinct came to him. He crawled quickly to where Philip lay and had him clean by the elbow.

The whole arm seemed red-hot, and the broken bone grated in the joint, sending out shoots of the essence of pain. His other arm was pinioned against the wall, and Gino had trampled in behind the stove and was kneeling on his legs. For the space of a minute he yelled and yelled with all the force of his lungs. Then this solace was denied him. The other hand, moist and strong, began to close round his throat.

At first he was glad, for here, he thought, was death at last. But it was only a new torture; perhaps

Gino inherited the skill of his ancestors—and child-like ruffians who flung each other from the towers. Just as the windpipe closed, the hand fell off, and Philip was revived by the motion of his arm. And just as he was about to faint and gain at last one moment of oblivion, the motion stopped, and he would struggle instead against the pressure on his throat.

Vivid pictures were dancing through the pain—Lilia dying some months back in this very house, Miss Abbott bending over the baby, his mother at home, now reading evening prayers to the servants. He felt that he was growing weaker; his brain wandered; the agony did not seem so great. Not all Gino's care could indefinitely postpone the end. His yells and gurgles became mechanical—functions of the tortured flesh rather than true notes of indignation and despair. He was conscious of a horrid tumbling. Then his arm was pulled a little too roughly, and everything was quiet at last.

"But your son is dead, Gino. Your son is dead, dear Gino. Your son is dead."

The room was full of light, and Miss Abbott had Gino by the shoulders, holding him down in a chair. She was exhausted with the struggle, and her arms were trembling.

"What is the good of another death? What is the good of more pain?"

He too began to tremble. Then he turned and looked curiously at Philip, whose face, covered with dust and foam, was visible by the stove. Miss Abbott allowed him to get up, though she still held him firmly. He gave a loud and curious cry—a cry of interrogation it might be called. Below there was the noise of Perfetta returning with the baby's milk.

"Go to him," said Miss Abbott, indicating Philip. "Pick him up. Treat him kindly."

She released him, and he approached Philip slowly. His eyes were filling with trouble. He bent down, as if he would gently raise him up.

"Help! help!" moaned Philip. His body had suffered too much from Gino. It could not bear to be touched by him.

Gino seemed to understand. He stopped, crouched above him. Miss Abbott herself came forward and lifted her friend in her arms.

"Oh, the foul devil!" he murmured. "Kill him! Kill him for me."

Miss Abbott laid him tenderly on the couch and wiped his face. Then she said gravely to them both, "This thing stops here."

"Latte! latte!" cried Perfetta, hilariously ascending the stairs.

"Remember," she continued, "there is to be no revenge. I will have no more intentional evil. We are not to fight with each other any more."

"I shall never forgive him," sighed Philip.

"Latte! latte freschissima! bianca come neve!" Perfetta came in with another lamp and a little jug.

Gino spoke for the first time. "Put the milk on the table," he said. "It will not be wanted in the other room." The peril was over at last. A great sob shook the whole body, another followed, and then he gave a piercing cry of woe, and stumbled towards Miss Abbott like a child and clung to her.

All through the day Miss Abbott had seemed to

Philip like a goddess, and more than ever did she seem so now. Many people look younger and more intimate during great emotion. But some there are who look older, and remote, and he could not think that there was little difference in years, and none in composition, between her and the man whose head was laid upon her breast. Her eyes were open, full of infinite pity and full of majesty, as if they discerned the boundaries of sorrow, and saw unimaginable tracts beyond. Such eyes he had seen in great pictures but never in a mortal. Her hands were folded round the sufferer, stroking him lightly, for even a goddess can do no more than that. And it seemed fitting, too, that she should bend her head and touch his forehead with her lips.

Philip looked away, as he sometimes looked away from the great pictures where visible forms suddenly become inadequate for the things they have shown to us. He was happy; he was assured that there was greatness in the world. There came to him an earnest desire to be good through the example of this good woman. He would try henceforward to be worthy of the things she had revealed. Quietly, without hysterical prayers or banging of drums, he underwent conversion. He was saved.

"That milk," said she, "need not be wasted. Take it, Signor Carella, and persuade Mr. Herriton to drink."

Gino obeyed her, and carried the child's milk to Philip. And Philip obeyed also and drank.

"Is there any left?"

"A little," answered Gino.

"Then finish it." For she was determined to use such remnants as lie about the world.

"Will you not have some?"

"I do not care for milk; finish it all."

"Philip, have you had enough milk?"

"Yes, thank you, Gino; finish it all."

He drank the milk, and then, either by accident or in some spasm of pain, broke the jug to pieces. Perfetta exclaimed in bewilderment. "It does not matter," he told her. "It does not matter. It will never be wanted any more."

Chapter Ten

"HE WILL HAVE to marry her," said Philip. "I heard from him this morning, just as we left Milan. He finds he has gone too far to back out. It would be expensive. I don't know how much he minds—not as much as we suppose, I think. At all events there's not a word of blame in the letter. I don't believe he even feels angry. I never was so completely forgiven. Ever since you stopped him killing me, it has been a vision of perfect friendship. He nursed me, he lied for me at the inquest, and at the funeral, though he was crying, you would have thought it was my son who had died. Certainly I was the only person he had to be kind to; he was so distressed not to make Harriet's acquaintance, and that he scarcely saw anything of you. In his letter he says so again."

"Thank him, please, when you write," said Miss Abbott, "and give him my kindest regards."

"Indeed I will." He was surprised that she could slide away from the man so easily. For his own part, he was bound by ties of almost alarming intimacy. Gino had the southern knack of friendship. In the intervals of business he would pull out Philip's life, turn it inside out, remodel it, and advise him how to use it for the best. The sensation was pleasant, for he was a kind as well as a skilful operator. But Philip came away feeling that he had not a secret corner left. In that very letter Gino had again implored him, as a refuge from domestic difficulties, "to marry Miss Abbott, even if her dowry is small." And how Miss Abbott herself, after such tragic intercourse, could resume the conventions and send calm messages of esteem, was more than he could understand.

"When will you see him again?" she asked. They were standing together in the corridor of the train, slowly ascending out of Italy towards the San Gothard tunnel.

"I hope next spring. Perhaps we shall paint Siena red for a day or two with some of the new wife's money. It was one of the arguments for marrying her."

"He has no heart," she said severely. "He does not really mind about the child at all."

"No; you're wrong. He does. He is unhappy, like the rest of us. But he doesn't try to keep up appearances as we do. He knows that the things that have made him happy once will probably make him happy again."

"He said he would never be happy again."

"In his passion. Not when he was calm. We

English say it when we are calm—when we do not really believe it any longer. Gino is not ashamed of inconsistency. It is one of the many things I like him for."

"Yes; I was wrong. That is so."

"He's much more honest with himself than I am," continued Philip, "and he is honest without an effort and without pride. But you, Miss Abbott, what about you? Will you be in Italy next spring?"

"No."

"I'm sorry. When will you come back, do you think?"

"I think never."

"For whatever reason?" He stared at her as if she were some monstrosity.

"Because I understand the place. There is no need."

"Understand Italy!" he exclaimed.

"Perfectly."

"Well, I don't. And I don't understand you," he murmured to himself, as he paced away from her up the corridor. By this time he loved her very much, and he could not bear to be puzzled. He had reached love by the spiritual path: her thoughts and her goodness and her nobility had moved him first, and now her whole body and all its gestures had become transfigured by them. The beauties that are called obvious—the beauties of her hair and her voice and her limbs—he had noticed these last; Gino, who never traversed any path at all, had commended them dispassionately to his friend.

Why was he so puzzling? He had known so

much about her once—what she thought, how she felt, the reasons for her actions. And now he only knew that he loved her, and all the other knowledge seemed passing from him just as he needed it most. Why would she never come to Italy again? Why had she avoided himself and Gino ever since the evening that she had saved their lives? The train was nearly empty. Harriet slumbered in a compartment by herself. He must ask her these questions now, and he returned quickly to her down the corridor.

She greeted him with a question of her own. "Are your plans decided?"

"Yes. I can't live at Sawston."

"Have you told Mrs. Herriton?"

"I wrote from Monteriano. I tried to explain things; but she will never understand me. Her view will be that the affair is settled—sadly settled since the baby is dead. Still it's over; our family circle need be vexed no more. She won't even be angry with you. You see, you have done us no harm in the long run. Unless, of course, you talk about Harriet and make a scandal. So that is my plan—London and work. What is yours?"

"Poor Harriet!" said Miss Abbott. "As if I dare judge Harriet! Or anybody." And without replying to Philip's question she left him to visit the other invalid.

Philip gazed after her mournfully, and then he looked mournfully out of the window at the decreasing streams. All the excitement was over—the inquest, Harriet's short illness, his own visit to the surgeon. He was convalescent, both in body and spirit, but convalescence brought no joy. In the looking-glass at the end of the corridor he saw his face haggard, and his shoulders pulled forward by the weight of the sling. Life was greater than he had supposed, but it was even less complete. He had seen the need for strenuous work and for righteousness. And now he saw what a very little way those things would go.

"Is Harriet going to be all right?" he asked. Miss Abbott had come back to him.

"She will soon be her old self," was the reply. For Harriet, after a short paroxysm of illness and remorse, was quickly returning to her normal state. She had been "thoroughly upset" as she phrased it, but she soon ceased to realize that anything was wrong beyond the death of a poor little child. Already she spoke of "this unlucky accident," and "the mysterious frustration of one's attempts to make things better." Miss Abbott had seen that she was comfortable, and had given her a kind kiss. But she returned feeling that Harriet, like her mother, considered the affair as settled.

"I'm clear enough about Harriet's future, and about parts of my own. But I ask again, What about yours?"

"Sawston and work," said Miss Abbott.

"No."

"Why not?" she asked, smiling.

"You've seen too much. You've seen as much and done more than I have."

"But it's so different. Of course I shall go to Sawston. You forget my father; and even if he wasn't there, I've a hundred ties: my district—I'm neglecting it shamefully—my evening classes, the St. James'———"

"Silly nonsense!" he exploded, suddenly moved to have the whole thing out with her. "You're too good—about a thousand times better than I am. You can't live in that hole; you must go among people who can hope to understand you. I mind for myself: I want to see you often—again and again."

"Of course we shall meet whenever you come down; and I hope that it will mean often."

"It's not enough; it'll only be in the old horrible way, each with a dozen relatives round us. No, Miss Abbott; it's not good enough."

"We can write at all events."

"You will write?" he cried, with a flush of pleasure. At times his hopes seemed so solid.

"I will indeed."

"But I say it's not enough—you can't go back to the old life if you wanted to. Too much has happened."

"I know that," she said sadly.

"Not only pain and sorrow, but wonderful things: that tower in the sunlight—do you remember it, and all you said to me? The theatre, even. And the next day—in the church; and our times with Gino."

"All the wonderful things are over," she said. "That is just where it is."

"I don't believe it. At all events not for me. The most wonderful things may be to come———"

"The wonderful things are over," she repeated, and looked at him so mournfully that he dare not contradict her. The train was crawling up the last ascent towards the Campanile of Airolo and the entrance of the tunnel.

"Miss Abbott," he murmured, speaking quickly, as if their free intercourse might soon be ended, "what is the matter with you? I thought I understood you, and I don't. All those two great first days at Monteriano I read you as clearly as you read me still. I saw why you had come, and why you changed sides, and afterwards I saw your wonderful courage and pity. And now you're frank with me one moment, as you used to be, and the next moment you shut me up. You see I owe too much to you—my life, and I don't know what besides. I won't stand it. You've gone too far to turn mysterious. I'll quote what you said to me: 'Don't be mysterious; there isn't the time.' I'll quote something else: 'I and my life must be where I live.' You can't live at Sawston."

He had moved her at last. She whispered to herself hurriedly. "It is tempting——" And those three words threw him into a tumult of joy. What was tempting to her? After all was the greatest of things possible? Perhaps, after long estrangement, after much tragedy, the South had brought them together in the end. That laughter in the theatre, those silver stars in the purple sky, even the violets of a departed spring, all had helped, and sorrow had helped also, and so had tenderness to others.

"It is tempting," she repeated, "not to be mysterious. I've wanted often to tell you, and then been afraid. I could never tell any one else, certainly no woman, and I think you're the one man who might understand and not be disgusted."

"Are you lonely?" he whispered. "Is it anything like that?"

"Yes." The train seemed to shake him towards her. He was resolved that though a dozen people were looking, he would yet take her in his arms. "I'm terribly lonely, or I wouldn't speak. I think you must know already." Their faces were crimson, as if the same thought was surging through them both.

"Perhaps I do." He came close to her. "Perhaps I could speak instead. But if you will say the word plainly you'll never be sorry; I will thank you for it all my life."

She said plainly "That I love him." Then she broke down. Her body was shaken with sobs, and lest there should be any doubt she cried between the sobs for Gino! Gino! Gino!

He heard himself remark "Rather! I love him too! When I can forget how he hurt me that evening. Though whenever we shake hands——" One of them must have moved a step or two, for when she spoke again she was already a little way apart.

"You've upset me." She stifled something that was perilously near hysterics. "I thought I was past all this. You're taking it wrongly. I'm in love with Gino—don't pass it off—I mean it crudely—you know what I mean. So laugh at me."

"Laugh at love?" asked Philip.

"Yes. Pull it to pieces. Tell me I'm a fool or worse—that he's a cad. Say all you said when Lilia fell in love with him. That's the help I want. I dare tell you this because I like you—and because you're without passion; you look on life as a spectacle; you don't enter it; you only find it funny or beautiful. So I can trust you to cure me. Mr. Herriton, isn't it funny?" She tried to laugh herself, but became frightened and had to stop. "He's not a gentleman, nor a Christian, nor good in any way. He's never flattered me nor honoured me. But because he's handsome, that's been enough. The son of an Italian dentist, with a pretty face." She repeated the phrase as if it was a charm against passion. "Oh, Mr. Herriton, isn't it funny!" Then, to his relief, she began to cry. "I love him, and I'm not ashamed of it. I love him, and I'm going to Sawston, and if I mayn't speak about him to you sometimes, I shall die."

In that terrible discovery Philip managed to think not of himself but of her. He did not lament. He did not even speak to her kindly, for he saw that she could not stand it. A flippant reply was what she asked and needed—something flippant and a little cynical. And indeed it was the only reply he could trust himself to make.

"Perhaps it is what the books call 'a passing fancy'?"

She shook her head. Even this question was too pathetic. For as far as she knew anything about herself, she knew that her passions, once aroused, were sure. "If I saw him often," she said, "I might remember what he is like. Or he might grow old. But I dare not risk it, so nothing can alter me now."

"Well, if the fancy does pass, let me know." After all, he could say what he wanted.

"Oh, you shall know quick enough."

"But before you retire to Sawston—are you so mighty sure?"

"What of?" She had stopped crying. He was treating her exactly as she had hoped.

"That you and he——" He smiled bitterly at the thought of them together. Here was the cruel antique malice of the gods, such as they once sent forth against Pasiphae. Centuries of aspiration and culture—and the world could not escape it. "I was going to say—whatever have you got in common?"

"Nothing except the times we have seen each other." Again her face was crimson. He turned his own face away.

"Which—which times?"

"The time I thought you weak and heedless, and went instead of you to get the baby. That began it, as far as I know the beginning. Or it may have begun when you took us to the theatre, and I saw him mixed up with music and light. But didn't understand till the morning. Then you opened the door—and I knew why I had been so happy. Afterwards, in the church, I prayed for us all; not for anything new, but that we might just be as we were—he with the child he loved, you and I and Harriet safe out of the place—and that I might never see him or speak to him again. I could have pulled through then—the thing was only coming near, like a wreath of smoke; it hadn't wrapped me round."

"But through my fault," said Philip solemnly, "he is parted from the child he loves. And because my life was in danger you came and saw him and spoke to him again." For the thing was even greater than she imagined. Nobody but himself would ever see round it now. And to see round it he was standing at an immense distance. He could even be glad that she had once held the beloved in her arms.

"Don't talk of 'faults.' You're my friend for ever, Mr. Herriton, I think. Only don't be charitable and shift or take the blame. Get over supposing I'm refined. That's what puzzles you. Get over that."

As he spoke she seemed to be transfigured, and to have indeed no part with refinement or unrefinement any longer. Out of this wreck there was revealed to him something indestructible—something which she, who had given it, could never take away.

"I say again, don't be charitable. If he had asked me, I might have given myself body and soul. That would have been the end of my rescue party. But all through he took me for a superior being—a goddess. I who was worshipping every inch of him, and every word he spoke. And that saved me."

Philip's eyes were fixed on the Campanile of Airolo. But he saw instead the fair myth of Endymion. This woman was a goddess to the end. For her no love could be degrading: she stood outside all degradation. This episode, which she thought so sordid, and which was so tragic for him, remained supremely beautiful. To such a height was he lifted, that without regret he could now have told her that he was her worshipper too. But what was the use of telling her? For all the wonderful things had happened.

"Thank you," was all that he permitted himself. "Thank you for everything."

She looked at him with great friendliness, for he had made her life endurable. At that moment the train entered the San Gothard tunnel. They hurried back to the carriage to close the windows lest the smuts should get into Harriet's eyes.